Leading in the Age of Intelligent Systems

by

Richard Lightcap, PhD

ISBN: 978-1-972154-05-2 (Paperback)
ISBN: 978-1-972154-04-5 (E-Book)

Library of Congress Control Number: 2026910005

Dedication

To Elizabeth, my beloved wife and enduring companion, whose presence has been the quiet strength beneath every page of this work. In uncertainty, you have been wisdom. In adversity, you have been my courage. Your steadfast faith has anchored my resolve while lifting my vision beyond what I believed possible.

This book is woven with threads of your patience and sacrifice. It was written in hours you guarded, in moments you steadied, and through seasons when perseverance required more than intellect alone. You have sheltered the silence where thought deepened, protected the hope that sustained it, and reminded me that purpose is never pursued alone.

If these pages carry any measure of clarity, conviction, or grace, they reflect what I have first received from you. This accomplishment stands not as an individual triumph but as a testament to partnership, devotion, and shared belief. To you, who transforms calling into courage and effort into enduring meaning.

Foreword: The Architect of the Digital Cathedral

by: Allen Spector, D.Sc.

Every era of leadership is defined by a central test. In one age, the challenge is industrial scale. In another, it is globalization. In another, it is digital transformation. The defining test of the present era is more complex and, in many ways, more consequential: how to lead wisely in a world increasingly shaped by intelligent systems.

For senior executives, public leaders, and institutional decision makers, the difficulty is no longer simply keeping pace with change. The deeper challenge is learning how to govern systems whose speed, autonomy, and complexity often exceed the assumptions on which traditional management was built. Across every sector, leaders are being asked to make strategic, ethical, and operational decisions in environments mediated by algorithms, automated workflows, distributed infrastructure, and opaque technical dependencies. These systems generate enormous capability, but capability without comprehension can quickly become risky.

That is why *Leading in the Age of Intelligent Systems* arrives at precisely the right moment.

This is not a book that treats technology as a side conversation for specialists. Nor is it a work content to offer fashionable language about innovation without confronting the deeper implications of the systems now shaping modern enterprise life. Instead, Dr. Lightcap presents a disciplined and necessary argument: leadership in the years ahead will depend on far more than vision, charisma, or managerial instinct. It will require leaders to understand enough of the underlying architecture of intelligent systems to govern their consequences responsibly.

That argument gives the book both its urgency and its value. The age of intelligent systems has changed the meaning of executive responsibility. Leaders are no longer simply accountable for people, capital, and strategy in the traditional sense. They are increasingly accountable for the behavior of systems they did not personally build, cannot always directly observe, and may not fully understand without deliberate effort. In such an environment, distance from technology is no longer a harmless executive convenience. It is a governance vulnerability.

One of the great strengths of this manuscript is its refusal to accept the false divide between technical rigor and human purpose. Dr. Lightcap moves with confidence through the realities of cloud architecture, automation, secure systems, governance, compliance, and digital trust. Yet the achievement of the book lies not only in its technical command. It lies in its insistence that the architecture of intelligent systems must always remain accountable to the institutions, people, and missions those systems are meant to serve.

That is a distinction of enormous importance. Many books in the technology and leadership space focus on what systems can do. Fewer pause long enough to ask what they should do, under whose authority they should operate, and what kind of leadership is necessary to ensure that intelligence at scale does not erode judgment, accountability, or institutional integrity. This work asks those harder questions, and it does so with seriousness.

The philosophical thread running through the book gives it an additional measure of depth. By drawing on Ecclesiastes as a moral counterweight to a culture obsessed with optimization, Dr. Lightcap reminds readers of something modern institutions are often tempted to forget: efficiency is not purpose, and acceleration is not wisdom. A system may be elegant, fast, and technically sophisticated, yet still move an enterprise away from the very ends leadership is meant to protect. If automation removes toil but also removes sovereignty, then progress has come at too high a price.

Readers will find, therefore, more than a guide to emerging technologies or enterprise platforms. They will find a framework for executive clarity. The book offers clarity in technical decision making, clarity in governance, clarity in compliance, and clarity in the role of human judgment within increasingly autonomous systems. Most importantly, it offers clarity about leadership itself. The central figure of the next decade will not be the passive overseer of systems built by others. It will be the architect-leader: the executive capable of aligning structure, accountability, resilience, and mission in an era when intelligence is increasingly embedded in the infrastructure of the institution.

That is why this book deserves careful attention from leaders across business, government, higher education, and professions. Its subject is not merely technology. Its subject is stewardship under new conditions of power. It addresses the reality that the systems now shaping organizations also shape trust, risk, legitimacy, and the future capacity of institutions to remain meaningfully human while operating at machine scale.

The most valuable books do more than describe a moment. They equip readers to meet it. *Leading in the Age of Intelligent Systems* does exactly that. It challenges leaders to move beyond superficial fluency and reclaim the kind of understanding required for genuine governance. It reminds them that intelligent systems do not diminish the need for leadership. They intensify it. And it makes a compelling case that the future will belong not to those who merely adopt the new tools of the age, but to those who can govern them with discipline, wisdom, and purpose.

The systems are running. The stakes are rising. Dr. Richard Lightcap has written a book for leaders prepared to meet that reality with seriousness equal to the task.

Contents

Part I: The Paradigm Shift

1: Beyond the Algorithm

The Magic Trick Is Over

In the early years of the 2020s, much of the world responded to artificial intelligence as though it were witnessing a magic trick. Large language models wrote poetry with startling fluency, generated functional software code in seconds, summarized complex research, and performed well enough on professional and academic exams to unsettle entire industries. What had once belonged to the realm of speculative fiction suddenly appeared on laptops, in boardrooms, and across enterprise platforms with a speed that few institutions were prepared to absorb. For leaders already navigating post pandemic instability, digital transformation pressure, workforce disruption, and rising competitive demands, the emergence of generative AI felt less like a technological milestone and more like an executive summons. A new force had arrived, and every serious organization believed it needed an answer.

That answer, in many cases, came quickly and superficially. Boards pressed chief executives to articulate an artificial intelligence strategy. Executive teams convened innovation councils. Vendors repackaged existing products with AI labels. Enterprises rolled out chatbots for customer support, bought enterprise licenses for generative assistants, and encouraged employees to experiment with prompt-based productivity. The prevailing assumption was simple: if intelligent models could write, summarize, recommend, and automate, then productivity gains would naturally follow. The technology itself was treated as the source of transformation. The model was assumed to be the strategy.

By 2026, however, the spell had begun to break. The novelty remained impressive, but novelty alone no longer carried strategic value. What once felt revolutionary quickly became accessible, replicable, and increasingly commoditized. Competing models began to converge in capability for many common enterprise use cases. Features that had seemed extraordinary became expected. In market after market, leaders discovered an uncomfortable truth: buying access to an algorithm was not the same as building institutional advantage. A generative model could produce elegant text, useful code, or persuasive analysis, but none of those outputs guaranteed business value, operational reliability, regulatory alignment, or strategic coherence.

The deeper realization was more significant than the fading of hype. The algorithm, while powerful, was never the whole story. In many cases, it was not even the most decisive part of the story. The real challenge was never simply whether a model could perform an impressive task in isolation. The real challenge was whether the organization could embed that capability into a trustworthy, resilient, governed, and mission aligned operating environment. A model could generate output, but it could not by itself establish data integrity, define accountability, redesign workflow, protect institutional sovereignty, or align automation with executive intent. Those responsibilities remained squarely within the domain of leadership.

This is where many organizations lost their footing. They treated AI as though it was a product acquisition problem rather than an architectural and leadership challenge. They focused on selecting the right engine while neglecting the system in which the engine would operate. They asked which model was smartest, fastest, or cheapest, while failing to ask whether their data was reliable, whether their workflows were mature, whether their controls were adequate, and whether their governance structures could absorb autonomous decision support at scale. In doing so, they mistook technical capability for organizational readiness.

The lesson for executives is now unavoidable. Leadership in the age of intelligent systems cannot be organized around fascination with the model alone. The era of being impressed by isolated demonstrations is over. The magic trick is over. What remains is the far more demanding work of design, integration, governance, and institutional stewardship. Leaders who continue to fixate on the algorithm itself will remain trapped in yesterday's conversation. Leaders who shift their attention from the engine to the machine, from isolated capability to systemic resilience, will be the ones prepared to lead what comes next.

To lead in this era, executives must learn to see beyond the algorithm.

The Component Versus the System

One of the most common mistakes modern leaders make is a category error. They speak about artificial intelligence as though it were a tool in the same class as a spreadsheet, a search engine, or a software feature that can be deployed, measured, and managed in isolation. This misunderstanding is understandable, particularly in organizations conditioned to think in terms of applications, licenses, and feature sets. Yet it is a dangerously incomplete way to understand what is actually happening. Artificial intelligence, when embedded into decision making, workflow, and enterprise infrastructure, is rarely just a tool. It is more accurately understood as one component within a broader system of interaction, dependency, control, and consequence.

That distinction matters because components can be purchased, but systems must be designed. Components can be switched on, but systems must be aligned. Components can impress during demonstrations, but systems must survive contact with reality. The leader who mistakes one for the other will consistently underestimate the demands of implementation and overestimate the value of the technology itself.

A useful analogy is the jet engine. On a test stand, a high-performance engine is a marvel of engineering. It represents precision, power, and highly refined capability. It can produce enormous thrust. Yet no serious observer would confuse an engine with an aircraft. Without an airframe, fuel systems, avionics, control surfaces, navigation architecture, maintenance protocols, and a pilot interface, the engine remains only a powerful component. In the absence of system integration, its power is not merely limited. It can become unstable, misdirected, or destructive. The engine becomes meaningful only when it is placed inside a larger architecture designed to convert force into controlled flight.

The same is true in the enterprise. An algorithm is a component. An intelligent system is an environment. The algorithm may perform the inferential work, generate the recommendation, classify the input, or produce the response. But its usefulness and trustworthiness depend entirely on the surrounding architecture in which it operates. The system includes the data that shapes its outputs, the workflows that translate outputs into action, the interfaces through which humans interpret and challenge its reasoning, and the governance structures that constrain its use. When leaders ignore these surrounding conditions, they do not simply misunderstand the technology. They create the conditions for fragility, drift, and failure.

In practical terms, an intelligent system in the enterprise is best understood as the integration of four distinct but interdependent layers.

The first is *data provenance*. This is the layer of origin, history, traceability, quality, and context. Every intelligent output rests upon the character of the data that informed it, whether through training, retrieval, prompting, fine tuning, or real time ingestion. Provenance asks foundational questions. Where did the data come from. Who created it. Under what conditions was it collected. Has it been altered, filtered, or corrupted. Does it represent institutional truth, stale assumptions, or contaminated noise. Without trustworthy provenance, the model's apparent intelligence becomes deceptive. It may produce elegant outputs based on incomplete, biased, or unverifiable inputs. In such cases, sophistication merely accelerates error.

The second layer is the *logic layer*, the algorithmic core. This is the inferential engine most people mean when they talk about AI. It is the layer that recognizes patterns, predicts outcomes, generates language, evaluates probabilities, or recommends actions. It matters greatly, but it does not operate in a vacuum. An organization can choose among different model architectures, sizes, vendors, and tuning approaches, yet even the most advanced model remains bound by the conditions around it. A powerful engine cannot rescue poorly designed aircraft. Likewise, an advanced model cannot compensate indefinitely for broken processes, unreliable data, weak oversight, or misaligned business intent.

The third layer is the *interface and workflow layer*. This is where intelligence becomes operational. It includes dashboards, prompts, integrations, approval chains, APIs, user experiences, escalation paths, and embedded process logic through which outputs move into human awareness and organizational action. This layer is often undervalued because it appears less glamorous than the model itself, yet it is frequently where success or failure is determined. An accurate recommendation delivered at the wrong time, in the wrong format, to the wrong person, without context or recourse, may be functionally useless. By contrast, a moderately capable model embedded in a well-designed workflow with clear human judgment points may create substantial and durable value. Workflow determines whether intelligence is merely generated or governed and applied.

The fourth layer is *governance guardrails*, including the disciplines of governance, risk, and compliance. This layer provides the structure that keeps intelligent systems from collapsing under the weight of their own autonomy. It defines authority, accountability, permissible use, oversight requirements, auditability, security expectations, ethical boundaries, and response mechanisms when things go wrong. Governance is what turns experimentation into stewardship.

It establishes not only what the system can do, but what it should do, who is responsible for its behavior, how exceptions are handled, and how trust is maintained over time. Without guardrails, intelligent systems tend to scale ambiguity, distribute risk, and automate consequences faster than institutions can interpret them.

When these four layers are properly aligned, the organization begins to operate not with an isolated AI tool, but with an intelligent system capable of supporting decision making in a resilient and mission aligned way. When they are misaligned, the result is often confusion disguised as innovation. Leaders may see promising demos and disappointing outcomes because the system beneath the demonstration was never mature enough to support real world use. The problem is then misdiagnosed as a weakness in the model, when in reality the failure was architectural.

This shift in perspective changes the questions leaders ask. Instead of asking, how smart is the AI, the better question becomes, how dependable is the ecosystem in which the AI operates. Instead of asking whether the model performs well in a controlled environment, leaders must ask whether the broader system can support accountability, transparency, and resilience under real conditions. Instead of asking which tool to buy, they must ask what institutional architecture is required to make intelligent capability trustworthy, governable, and strategically useful.

That is the beginning of executive maturity in the age of intelligent systems. The objective is not to admire the component. The objective is to govern the system.

The End of the Black Box Era

For years, one of the most convenient defenses in technology leadership was the language of the black box. When an intelligent system produced a biased recommendation, exposed a security weakness, generated a flawed compliance output, or made a decision that no one could easily explain, leaders often retreated to the same answer: the model is a black box. Its internal logic is too complex to interpret fully. The system has produced an unexpected result, but the mechanism behind the result cannot be meaningfully unpacked. In earlier phases of digital transformation, that explanation was often tolerated. Complexity itself was treated as a kind of institutional shield. If the system was advanced enough, opacity was assumed to be unavoidable.

That era is over.

By 2026, regulators, boards, shareholders, auditors, employees, and customers have grown far less patient with algorithmic mystery. Institutions can no longer invoke technical opacity as a defense against accountability. The public has now seen enough examples of automated harm, biased outputs, fragile integrations, security failures, and poorly governed autonomous behavior to recognize a central truth: when leaders deploy systems that affect people, decisions, rights, money, safety, or trust, the inability to explain those systems is not a technical footnote. It is a governance failure. The question is no longer whether a model is complex. The question is whether the organization has built sufficient visibility, control, and oversight around that complexity to govern its consequences responsibly.

This marks a profound shift in executive responsibility. Leadership in the age of intelligent systems is no longer satisfied by performance metrics alone. A system may appear effective according to speed, cost, or throughput and still represent an unacceptable leadership failure if its operations cannot be understood well enough to evaluate risk, intervene when needed, and defend its use under scrutiny. Institutions are now expected to demonstrate more than innovation. They are expected to demonstrate accountable innovation. That means leaders must be able to explain not every microscopic detail of a model's internal mathematics, but the broader logic of the system as it functions within the enterprise.

This is an important distinction. No executive is required to comprehend every parameter of a large neural network or personally reverse engineer every probabilistic behavior within an advanced model. That is not the standard. The standard is more practical and more demanding at the same time. Leaders must understand the anatomy of system behavior well enough to answer foundational questions. What data enters the system. How is it filtered, transformed, and prioritized. What assumptions shape its outputs. What workflows convert output into action. What thresholds trigger human review. What controls limit the blast radius of failure. What mechanisms exist to pause, override, escalate, or terminate automated behavior when risk begins to accumulate. These are not merely technical questions. They are leadership questions.

The shift from model accountability to systemic accountability is one of the defining governance changes of the intelligent systems era. It is not enough to say the model performed well in testing. It is not enough to say the vendor is reputable. It is not enough to say the team followed emerging best practices. If the system is sufficiently consequential to influence hiring, lending, patient care, compliance decisions, cybersecurity response, financial recommendations, public communications, or strategic direction, then its logic must be governable even if its internals remain mathematically complex. Responsible leadership requires the ability to explain how the system operates in context, where its vulnerabilities lie, and what safeguards stand between intelligent automation and institutional harm.

This is where many executives make a costly mistake. They assume that opacity is an unavoidable characteristic of advanced systems and therefore outside the practical reach of leadership. In reality, the critical issue is not whether the algorithmic core is partially opaque. The critical issue is whether the organization has chosen to surround that core with sufficient transparency in everything around it. Inputs can be governed. Interfaces can be designed for review. Workflow transitions can be instrumented. Escalation paths can be defined. Overrides can be implemented. Logs can be preserved. Approval rights can be assigned. Exposure can be limited. Even when the model is not fully interpretable at a microscopic level, the system can still be made visible enough to be managed responsibly.

That principle leads to what may be called the architect's axiom: complexity is never an excuse for the absence of control. Complexity may require new forms of oversight, but it does not remove the obligation to establish them. Leaders are not called to eliminate every unknown. They are called to design institutions in which unknowns are bounded, monitored, and made governable. The task is not to pretend that advanced systems are simple. The task is to ensure that complexity does not become a hiding place for negligence.

The black box, then, must be reframed. The objective is not always to open every layer of algorithmic reasoning and make it intuitively legible to every stakeholder. In many cases, that goal is unrealistic. The executive obligation is instead to place the black box inside a glass cage of visibility. That glass cage is constructed through architecture, auditability, governance, role clarity, policy enforcement, and operational instrumentation. It allows leaders to observe flows, track decisions, test assumptions, identify anomalies, and intervene before the system's speed outruns institutional judgment.

This is the new threshold of credible leadership. If a leader cannot explain how an intelligent system reaches action, what data and controls shape it, and how the organization maintains authority over its operation, then leadership has already fallen behind the technology it claims to govern. In the age of intelligent systems, opacity is no longer a defense. It is a warning.

The Anatomy of Intelligence: From Ingestion to Action

To lead beyond the algorithm, executives must learn to trace the nervous system of the modern enterprise. Intelligent systems do not merely produce outputs in isolation. They move through a chain of activity that begins with information intake and ends in action, consequence, and institutional memory. That chain is often invisible to nontechnical leaders because it unfolds at machine speed across multiple environments, applications, and decision points. Yet if leadership is to remain meaningful, that lifecycle must become conceptually visible. The ability to understand how intelligence flows through an organization is now as important as the ability to read a balance sheet, interpret a risk report, or evaluate an operating model.

At a high level, intelligent systems follow a predictable lifecycle, even if the technical implementations vary. That lifecycle usually includes ingestion, inference, orchestration, and auditability. Each stage carries its own operational value, risk exposure, and leadership implications. Weaknesses at any stage can degrade the quality, trustworthiness, or safety of everything that follows. Strength at each stage creates the conditions for intelligent systems to become not only powerful, but dependable.

The first stage is *ingestion*. This is the moment when the system receives the raw material from which later outputs will be shaped. Data may be pulled from cloud platforms such as Azure or AWS, from enterprise applications, local databases, identity systems, endpoint telemetry, GRC platforms, customer records, document repositories, or real time event streams. In some environments, ingestion also includes external feeds, third party APIs, regulatory updates, or retrieval pipelines that supply contextual knowledge to a model at runtime. Because ingestion sits at the front of the lifecycle, it is easy to underestimate how consequential it is. In truth, ingestion is where many later failures are born.

If the system ingests stale data, unverified records, biased samples, incomplete inventories, duplicate entries, mislabeled content, or compromised sources, then intelligence is poisoned at the source. The model may still produce polished outputs, but polished outputs do not guarantee truthful ones. In this sense, ingestion is not a clerical step. It is an epistemic step. It determines what the system is allowed to treat as reality. A leadership team that ignores ingestion discipline effectively delegates truth formation to whichever data sources happen to be most accessible, cheapest, or fastest to connect. That is not intelligence. It is automation built on unexamined assumptions.

The second stage is *inference*. This is the layer most closely associated with artificial intelligence in the public imagination. Here the model evaluates data, recognizes patterns, predicts outcomes, generates text, classifies events, scores risk, recommends actions, or produces a response based on the parameters, tuning choices, retrieval context, and constraints defined by system designers. Inference is where the algorithmic engine does its work. It is the point at which raw input is converted into machine judgment.

Yet even here, leadership must resist oversimplification. Inference is not just a technical event. It is a policy carrying event. Every model reflects embedded assumptions about relevance, priority, confidence, weighting, and permissible response space. A recommendation engine deciding what to elevate, a compliance assistant determining what appears material, or a security model prioritizing certain threat indicators over others is never neutral in any practical sense.

Inference expresses hidden decisions about what matters, what is ignored, and what the organization has chosen to privilege. For that reason, leaders must understand that model behavior is never detached from institutional values. It operationalizes them, whether intentionally or accidentally.

The third stage is *orchestration*. This is where the system moves from intelligence to consequence. A model does not create organizational value merely by generating an output. Value emerges when that output is translated into action inside a workflow. Orchestration is the connective tissue that makes that translation possible. It may trigger an API call, open a ticket, update a GRC portal, reroute traffic, deny a transaction, issue a compliance alert, populate a dashboard, notify a human reviewer, or initiate a downstream process without further manual intervention. Orchestration is, in effect, the bridge between machine reasoning and institutional behavior.

This stage deserves special executive attention because it is where risk begins to compound rapidly. An inaccurate output that remains visible for human review is one kind of problem. An inaccurate output that is automatically operationalized across interconnected systems is another kind entirely. Orchestration determines how much autonomy the organization is willing to grant the system, under what conditions, and with what safeguards. It defines where human judgment enters, where escalation occurs, where action is delayed pending approval, and where automated behavior may proceed at machine speed. In many enterprises, the greatest value from intelligent systems is unlocked here, but so are the greatest dangers. The transition from inference to orchestration is where intelligence becomes power.

The fourth stage is *auditability*. Every meaningful action within an intelligent system must leave a digital footprint that is durable, searchable, attributable, and context rich. Auditability is what allows institutions to reconstruct events, explain system behavior, identify control failures, validate compliance, investigate anomalies, and learn from outcomes. Without it, the organization may have intelligence in motion but no reliable memory of how that intelligence moved. In such an environment, failures become difficult to diagnose, accountability becomes diffused, and leadership loses the ability to govern retrospectively, which in turn weakens its ability to govern prospectively.

Auditability is not only a compliance concern. It is a strategic discipline. It allows an organization to determine whether its systems are producing value in the way intended, whether certain pathways create recurring errors, whether specific interventions reduce harm, and whether human oversight is functioning as designed. It is how trust scales beyond personality and anecdote. A system that cannot be audited may still be fast and impressive, but it cannot be considered mature.

Leadership, therefore, does not reside in any single stage of the lifecycle. It resides in the intersections between them. It is found in the decisions about what data may enter the system and under what conditions. It is found in the assumptions embedded into inferential logic. It is found in the workflow rules that determine whether output remains advisory or becomes operational. It is found in the logs, controls, reviews, and retention structures that make actions visible after the fact. The executive task is to ensure those intersections are intentional, aligned, and governable.

Among all these transitions, the movement from inference to orchestration is often the most consequential. It is the moment when a model's internal judgment begins to shape real world outcomes. It is where a recommendation becomes a workflow event, where classification becomes prioritization, where generated language becomes customer communication, where anomaly detection becomes enforcement, and where predicted risk becomes operational action. If the organization has designed this transition well, intelligent systems can accelerate responsiveness, improve precision, reduce toil, and strengthen decision support. If the transition is poorly governed, the same systems can scale error, ambiguity, and institutional exposure with extraordinary efficiency.

To lead intelligently, then, is not merely to admire what the system can infer. It is to understand how that inference becomes action, how that action becomes consequence, and how those consequences remain visible to the institution that authorized them. That is the anatomy of intelligence in the enterprise. And that is where real leadership begins.

The Digital Organism: A New Teammate

The enterprise is moving beyond the era of software as a service and into something more dynamic, more adaptive, and more consequential. For years, organizations thought of software primarily as a toolset: a platform to support accounting, customer service, communications, analytics, or operations. The relationship was largely transactional. Humans issued commands. Software executed functions. Even complex platforms were still understood as instruments, inert until directed by a user. That mental model is now becoming insufficient.

Intelligent systems are beginning to behave less like static tools and more like active participants within the life of the institution. They retrieve information, generate language, recommend next steps, trigger workflows, escalate events, monitor anomalies, synthesize patterns, and increasingly interact with both humans and other systems in ways that resemble delegated agency. While these systems are not alive in the biological sense, they do occupy a new functional role. They are persistent, responsive, adaptive, and increasingly embedded in the rhythm of organizational life. In that respect, they begin to resemble something closer to a digital organism than a conventional application.

This shift matters because leadership habits formed in the software era do not automatically translate into the age of intelligent systems. A conventional tool does not require cultural integration. A spreadsheet does not need supervision, boundaries, or a feedback loop. An intelligent system does. Once a system begins shaping workflow, influencing judgment, and participating in institutional action, the organization must think differently about how it is introduced, monitored, corrected, and aligned. It becomes not merely a technical asset, but a functional presence inside the enterprise.

A useful way to understand this change is to think in terms of teammates. No responsible leader would hire a new employee, assign meaningful authority, and then provide no reporting structure, no boundaries, no performance expectations, no review process, and no recourse when performance begins to drift. Yet this is precisely how many organizations have deployed artificial intelligence. Systems are given access to sensitive data, embedded into consequential workflows, and allowed to influence communications or decisions without sufficient oversight, role clarity, or behavioral guardrails. The result is not innovation. It is unmanaged delegation.

The leadership task in this environment is not domination, but curation. Intelligent systems cannot simply be installed and forgotten. They must be observed, shaped, constrained, and continuously evaluated in light of changing conditions. Their behavior must be tested against mission. Their outputs must be interpreted in context. Their authority must remain conditional rather than assumed. Their integration must be treated as an ongoing act of institutional design. This is what may be called curatorial oversight.

Curatorial oversight represents a more mature model of executive responsibility. It assumes that leadership is no longer limited to managing people or monitoring isolated outputs. Instead, leadership becomes the disciplined work of managing intent across an ecosystem in which human and machine agencies are increasingly intertwined. The central question shifts. Leaders no longer ask only how much work was produced or how quickly a task was completed. They ask whether the system remains aligned with institutional purpose. They ask whether automation is reinforcing mission or gradually distorting it. They ask whether speed is being gained at the expense of judgment, whether convenience is eroding accountability, and whether the system's behavior still reflects the values the institution claims to hold.

This is a subtler and more demanding form of leadership than traditional output management. It requires attention not only to performance, but to orientation. An intelligent system may be highly productive and still be strategically misaligned. It may reduce labor and still degrade trust. It may improve throughput and still weaken human capability if it gradually displaces expertise rather than augmenting it. Curatorial oversight therefore requires leaders to remain close to the evolving relationship between system behavior and institutional intent.

Seen in this light, the intelligent system is neither merely a servant nor a threat. It is a new kind of organizational participant, one that must be governed with clarity, humility, and discipline. The leader's role is not to anthropomorphize the machine, but to recognize that once agency is delegated into technical infrastructure, leadership must expand to include the stewardship of that delegated agency. That is the beginning of maturity in the age of digital organisms.

The Vanity of the Algorithm

One of the most persistent temptations in the age of intelligent systems is the temptation of novelty. Every cycle of innovation brings a new promise: a larger model, a faster model, a more efficient architecture, a cheaper inference path, a more impressive benchmark, a new frontier in multimodal capability, a fresh claim that the next release changes everything. For executives under pressure to remain competitive, responsive, and future ready, the attraction is understandable. No leader wants to be the one who underestimated a genuine inflection point. No board wants to discover that strategic hesitation became institutional decline.

Yet there is a profound difference between responsiveness and restlessness. The pursuit of the newest system can easily become a form of executive vanity, especially when technological adoption is severed from architectural readiness and organizational purposes. In such cases, institutions begin to confuse motion with progress. They spend aggressively on premium models, adopt tools at speed, announce transformation initiatives, and celebrate technical capability without first establishing visibility, control, accountability, or mission coherence. What appears to be innovation is often only acceleration without direction.

Ancient wisdom offers a fitting frame for this problem. Toil without purpose is chasing after the wind. The phrase captures with striking precision the condition of many modern enterprises. They are moving quickly, investing heavily, and producing an extraordinary volume of activity, yet they cannot clearly explain what enduring value is being built or what governing logic holds the pieces together. In such an environment, the algorithm becomes an object of fascination rather than a disciplined instrument of strategy.

An organization that spends millions on the latest large language model while lacking centralized workflow visibility, coherent policy enforcement, meaningful audit trails, or integrated governance has not built intelligence in any mature sense. It has simply installed a more powerful engine in a vehicle that cannot be steered with confidence.

The system may move faster. It may even impress observers in the short term. But speed without direction amplifies exposure rather than advantage. Intelligence without governance magnifies ambiguity rather than clarity.

This is why executive leadership beyond the algorithm requires a deeper form of discernment. Leaders must learn to distinguish capability from readiness. A model may be state of the art, but the institution may still be structurally unprepared to use it well. A system may demonstrate remarkable performance in isolated testing yet fail to create trusted value because the surrounding workflows are fragmented, the data is contested, the controls are weak, and the reporting lines are unclear. Without governance, even technical excellence becomes unstable.

The issue is not whether advanced models matter. They do. The issue is whether organizations mistake raw capability for strategic sufficiency. The algorithm provides power, but power alone is never enough. In every durable institution, power must be ordered by purpose. It must be bound by accountability. It must be made legible to those charged with stewardship. It must serve a mission larger than itself. That is why governance is not a bureaucratic afterthought attached to innovation after deployment. Governance is what gives intelligent capability shape, legitimacy, and direction. It is what turns computational force into institutional value.

For leaders, then, the challenge is not to reject the algorithm, but to resist becoming mesmerized by it. The task is to see clearly in an environment designed to reward fascination. Clarity is now a competitive advantage. It allows the executive to ask harder and more useful questions. Does this capability reinforce our mission. Does it strengthen trust. Does it improve resilience. Does it increase our capacity for judgment rather than erode it. Do we have the architectural maturity to govern what we are about to deploy. These questions matter more than benchmark scores, release announcements, or vendor demonstrations because they force the organization to reconnect technical possibilities with institutional meaning.

True leadership in the age of intelligent systems is therefore not defined by the speed with which new models are acquired. It is defined by the discipline with which power is placed in service of purpose. Beyond the algorithm lies the real work of leadership: the recovery of clarity in the midst of complexity, and the insistence that governance is not the enemy of innovation, but the condition that makes worthy innovation possible.

Conclusion: The Path Ahead

The argument of this chapter has been straightforward, but its implications are far reaching. Artificial intelligence, impressive as it may be, is only one component within a much larger enterprise reality. The real strategic prize is not the algorithm in isolation, but the intelligent system as a whole. That system includes data provenance, inferential logic, workflow integration, orchestration, auditability, and governance. It includes the structures that make intelligence usable, visible, and trustworthy. It includes the leadership discipline required to ensure that technical capability remains aligned with human purpose and institutional accountability.

The age of the magic trick has passed. Organizations can no longer afford to be mesmerized by isolated demonstrations of machine fluency. The novelty has worn off, and what remains is the harder, more consequential work of architecture. Leaders must now understand how intelligent systems are assembled, how they act, how they fail, and how they can be governed under real conditions. They must move beyond curiosity about outputs and toward responsibility for outcomes. They must learn to see not only what the system can produce, but what the system is becoming inside the life of the institution.

This shift carries with it a deeper question of identity. If leaders are no longer simply managers of people who use tools, then what are they becoming? As delegated agency moves steadily from human actors into digital environments, the role of leadership must evolve accordingly. The enterprise is undergoing a silent handover in which increased judgment, coordination, prioritization, and action are being mediated by machines. In such a moment, the leader cannot remain a distant overseer. A new type of executive identity is beginning to emerge, one shaped less by supervision alone and more by design, stewardship, and systemic accountability.

That new identity is the subject of the next chapter. There, attention will turn from the system itself to the leader required to govern it. The question is no longer whether institutions will adopt intelligent systems. The question is whether the people charged with guiding those institutions are prepared to become what the age now demands: architect-leaders.

2: The Architect-Leader

The Identity Crisis of the Modern Manager

For more than a century, the definition of a good manager remained remarkably stable. Across industries, organizations rewarded leaders who could align people, allocate resources, monitor performance, and deliver results within a defined period of time. The manager was expected to motivate, coordinate, correct, and occasionally discipline. At times, the role resembled that of a coach, drawing out the best from a team through encouragement and development. At other times, it resembled that of a talent scout, identifying strengths, filling gaps, and positioning people where they could contribute most effectively. In more difficult moments, it resembled that of a policeman, enforcing standards, resolving conflict, and ensuring that expectations were met. Though the style varied, the underlying structure remained the same. Managers led people, and people used tools.

That hierarchy shaped nearly every major leadership model of the modern enterprise. Work was understood as a largely human activity supported by technology. Tools amplified labor, but they did not meaningfully rival the human worker as a source of judgment, creativity, pattern recognition, or operational decision making. Even highly advanced systems were treated as subordinate instruments. The core assumption beneath managerial practice was therefore simple: if leaders could organize human effort effectively, the organization would perform.

That assumption is now under pressure.

In the age of intelligent systems, the traditional relationship between leaders, workers, and tools has begun to collapse. Organizations now operate in environments where core functions are increasingly mediated by systems that do more than assist. They analyze, generate, recommend, prioritize, escalate, orchestrate, and, in some cases, act with limited autonomy inside enterprise workflows. A cluster of agents running across cloud infrastructure may now produce more code in a day than a small team once produced in a week. A decision support system may surface patterns that no analyst would have identified at human speed. A workflow engine may route, classify, and respond to events without waiting for direct supervision. In such an environment, the most productive contributor is no longer always a person, and the most consequential work is no longer always visible at the level of individual human effort.

This creates an identity crisis for the modern manager. Many leadership instincts formed in an earlier era still assume that performance is best governed through human centered practices alone. The organization schedules one on ones, calibrates performance reviews, builds team culture, and refines communication norms, all of which still matter. But these practices now operate alongside systems whose behavior is shaped less by motivation than by architecture. An autonomous workflow does not respond to inspiration. A model driven process has not improved because it received developmental feedback in a quarterly check-in. A recommendation engine will not become more aligned simply because the team culture is healthy. Those forms of leadership remain important, but they are no longer sufficient to govern the environments in which value is increasingly created.

This is the decisive shift. Leaders are no longer only supervising work. They are designing the conditions under which work happens. The center of gravity has moved from direct oversight of human output to the intentional structuring of environments in which human and machine agencies interact. The leader's responsibility is no longer exhausted by asking whether people are performing well. It now includes asking whether the systems around those people are configured in ways that support trust, resilience, accountability, and mission. Leadership becomes less about monitoring visible effort and more about shaping invisible architecture.

That transition demands a different professional identity. The next generation of executive leadership cannot be built solely on the assumptions of classical management. The leader who thrives in this era must still understand people, incentives, communication, and institutional culture. But that leader must also understand design, governance, dependency, workflow, and systemic consequences. The role is no longer limited to managing teams that use tools. It is increasingly defined by governing environments in which tools have become participants in the production of outcomes.

This is the rise of the architect-leader.

The architect-leader does not abandon human leadership. On the contrary, human leadership becomes more important precisely because intelligent systems increase the scale, speed, and complexity of what organizations can do. But the nature of that leadership changes. The architect-leader must think structurally. The architect-leader must ask how decisions move, where risk accumulates, how authority is delegated, what assumptions are embedded into workflows, and how institutional values are translated into technical constraints. While the traditional manager focused on directing activity, the architect-leader focuses on designing conditions. While earlier forms of leadership were often judged by how effectively they managed execution, the new standard is increasing whether the leader can build an environment in which execution remains aligned, governable, and worthy of trust.

This is not a cosmetic adjustment to leadership vocabulary. It is a redefinition of executive responsibility. Institutions do not merely need better managers for intelligent systems. They need leaders capable of understanding that management itself has entered a new age. The question is no longer only whether teams are effective. The question is whether the architecture within which teams and systems operate has been designed well enough to make effective performance possible. That is the beginning of the -eader's work.

From Managing Output to Governing Logic

Traditional leadership is largely reactive in structure, even when it is proactive in aspiration. A manager typically waits for work to take shape, then evaluates what has been produced. A report is submitted. A line of code is written. A proposal is drafted. A sales call is completed. A product decision is made. Only after the output exists does the manager step in to assess quality, provide feedback, approve changes, or redirect effort. This model made sense in environments where work moved at human speed and where most consequential decisions were still visibly tethered to identifiable individuals.

That sequence no longer holds in an intelligent system. Outputs may now be generated in milliseconds, propagated across platforms instantly, and translated into downstream actions before any human reviewer has time to interpret what happened. A recommendation engine may reprioritize cases in real time. A model driven workflow may classify risk, trigger notifications, or update records automatically. An automated assistant may generate communications, documentation, or decision support artifacts at a scale that outpaces conventional review practices. In such an environment, waiting for output before exercising leadership is often equivalent to surrendering control. By the time the leader reacts, the decision may already have moved, the workflow may already have been executed, and the consequences may already be unfolding.

This is why the architect-leader moves upstream.

The fundamental shift is from managing outputs to governing the logic that produces them. Instead of concentrating leadership attention only on what emerges at the end of a process, the architect-leader focuses on the structures, rules, inputs, dependencies, and permissions that shape what the system is capable of generating in the first place. The leadership question changes from whether the final artifact appears acceptable to whether the conditions that produced the artifact are properly designed, governed, and aligned with institutional purpose.

The difference may appear subtle at first, but it is profound in practice. A traditional manager might ask whether a report is accurate, well written, or useful. Those questions remain valid, but they occur late in the chain. The architect-leader asks a prior set of questions. What data sources fed the report. Were those sources current, authorized, and contextually appropriate. What compliance parameters shaped, retrieval and synthesis. What workflow rules determined how the report was generated, who reviewed it, and where it was sent. What thresholds were established for escalation. What assumptions were embedded into the system's treatment of confidence, risk, or materiality. In other words, the architect-leader is not satisfied merely by reviewing the visible product. The architect-leader seeks to govern the invisible machinery that made the product possible.

This upstream orientation is one of the defining characteristics of leadership in the age of intelligent systems. When outputs arrive at machine speed, the most consequential leadership decisions must occur before those outputs exist. They occur when data pipelines are selected, when permissions are granted, when governance rules are defined, when workflow transitions are configured, and when human review points are either embedded or omitted. These are not secondary implementation details. They are acts of leadership. They express what the organization values, what risks it is willing to tolerate, how it allocates authority, and where it insists on maintaining human judgment.

Seen this way, logic gates are not merely technical features. They are institutional commitments rendered operational.

Every filter, threshold, routing rule, escalation trigger, confidence score, approval requirement, and kill switch reflects a choice about how intelligence will behave inside the organization. Those choices determine whether the system reinforces accountability or obscures it, strengthens resilience or introduces fragility, accelerates mission or undermines it. The architect-leader understands that governance is not imposed after the system is built. Governance is built into the system by design.

This does not eliminate the importance of human conversation, coaching, or review. It reframes where those practices fit. The conference room remains important, but it is no longer the only site of leadership. Increasingly, leadership occurs in design sessions, architecture reviews, policy decisions, workflow mapping exercises, data governance discussions, and control validation efforts. It occurs when leaders insist that provenance matters before performance can be trusted. It occurs when they require that autonomous behavior be bounded before it is scaled. It occurs when they design systems in which speed serves judgment rather than outrunning it.

The architect-leader therefore becomes a governor of preconditions. The task is not merely to inspect what the system has done, but to shape what the system is allowed to do, how it does it, and under what oversight conditions it may proceed. This is a more demanding responsibility than traditional output review because it requires structural thinking. It requires the leader to understand that the most important decision may not be whether a single output passes inspection, but whether the environment producing thousands of outputs each day is architecturally sound.

That is the deeper meaning of moving upstream. The architect-leader recognizes that in intelligent environments, the decisive point of control lies not at the end of the workflow, but at its design. Leadership becomes less about correcting results after the fact and more about constructing systems in which results are more likely to be trustworthy from the beginning. The quality of the output still matters, but the governing logic behind the output matters more, because it is the logic that will determine whether quality can scale, whether risk can be contained, and whether the institution remains accountable for what its systems are doing in its name.

The Three Pillars of Architectural Leadership

If the defining task of the modern leader is no longer merely to supervise outputs but to govern the systems that produce them, then a new set of executive competencies becomes essential. Many of these responsibilities were once treated as highly technical matters and delegated downward into information technology, security, or engineering teams. That division no longer holds. In the age of intelligent systems, the architecture of digital decision making has become inseparable from executive strategy. The leader who does not understand the structural foundations of system behavior will eventually be forced to govern consequences without having shaped causes.

Architectural leadership, at its core, rests on three interdependent pillars: parameter design, workflow orchestration, and systems telemetry. Together, these pillars determine whether intelligent systems remain aligned with organizational intent, bounded by risk tolerance, and visible enough to be governed responsibly over time. They are not simply technical domains. They are the operating disciplines through which leadership becomes durable in an environment increasingly defined by automated judgment and delegated agency.

The first pillar is *parameter design*, the deliberate shaping of system guardrails. Every intelligent system operates within boundaries, whether those boundaries are explicit or assumed. Models are constrained through prompts, thresholds, permissions, confidence levels, policy instructions, escalation triggers, content restrictions, model selection logic, and access controls. These choices determine what the system is allowed to do, what it is prohibited from doing, how much latitude it has in ambiguous situations, and when it must defer to human authority. If the boundaries are too loose, the system may become unstable, insecure, biased, or operationally reckless. It may hallucinate, expose sensitive information, violate policy, or act in ways that outpace institutional tolerance for risk. If the boundaries are too restrictive, the system may become technically safe but strategically irrelevant, too constrained to create value, too hesitant to support decision making, and too cumbersome to be adopted in real work.

This is why parameter design is not a narrow implementation detail. It is an act of leadership. It is the place where institutional risk appetite is translated into operational logic. It is where executives decide, whether directly or through delegated authority, how much autonomy a system should possess, where discretion should end, which forms of uncertainty require escalation, and what kinds of behavior are incompatible with organizational purpose. In a very real sense, parameter design is how a leader encodes culture into the operating environment. It teaches the system what kinds of action are acceptable, what kinds are discouraged, and what kinds are forbidden. Just as a healthy institutional culture guides human judgment through norms and boundaries, well designed parameters guide machine behavior through constraints that reflect mission, accountability, and trust.

The second pillar is *workflow orchestration*, the design of the pathways through which intelligence moves into action. If parameter design defines the limits of system behavior, orchestration determines how that behavior travels through the enterprise. It governs the sequence of events by which data is received, interpreted, routed, approved, acted upon, escalated, and recorded. In traditional organizations, workflow was often treated as an operational matter, a process map to support handoffs between people and departments. In intelligent systems, workflow becomes a strategic concern because it determines whether autonomy remains supervised, whether risk is checked before it compounds, and whether machine speed is harnessed in a way that preserves institutional judgment.

Autonomy should never be confused with the absence of supervision. Mature autonomy is always structured. It operates within pathways designed for oversight, intervention, and accountability. This is where governance, risk, and compliance must be reimagined. In too many institutions, GRC is still treated as an external constraint applied after innovation has already begun. The architect-leader understands the opposite. Governance is not a hurdle, placed in front of progress. It is a design feature embedded directly into the workflow so that every meaningful autonomous action is paired with the appropriate level of review, policy enforcement, or control verification. A workflow that automatically checks permissions before action, verifies policy thresholds before release, triggers review when confidence falls below a set level, or preserves mandatory records for later inquiry is not slowed by governance. It is strengthened by it.

This is the executive opportunity hidden within orchestration. By designing workflows intentionally, leaders can ensure that intelligent systems do not operate as isolated pockets of technical capability but as governed instruments of enterprise purpose. The question is no longer simply whether the system can act. The question is whether it acts through a pathway that makes its behavior reliable, explainable, and accountable at scale.

The third pillar is *systems telemetry*, the discipline of making intelligent behavior visible in real time. No architect would trust the integrity of a complex structure based on hope or intuition alone. Buildings are governed through plans, inspections, load calculations, stress monitoring, maintenance records, and, where necessary, structural sensors that reveal when conditions begin to change. Intelligent systems require the same principle. Leaders cannot govern what they cannot see. If system behavior remains hidden until failure becomes public, then leadership has already ceded the advantage.

Systems telemetry provides the visibility necessary for observability. It shows how intelligent agents are performing, how workflows are behaving, where delays or anomalies are emerging, where error rates are increasing, where outputs are drifting from expected patterns, and where system behavior is beginning to separate from original intent. This is not about micromanagement. It is about maintaining sufficient situational awareness to distinguish healthy adaptation from dangerous drift. A leader does not need to stare at every event or intervene in every decision. But the leader must ensure that the institution has the capacity to observe system behavior at the level necessary to govern it.

This is why so many organizations now seek what is often called a single pane of glass: a unified operational view through which system health, workflow status, risk indicators, control effectiveness, and agent performance can be monitored in an integrated way. Such visibility is not merely convenient. It is increasingly foundational to executive stewardship. Without it, leadership becomes fragmented, reactive, and dependent on delayed reporting. With it, leadership becomes more anticipatory, more disciplined, and more capable of aligning system behavior with institutional intent over time.

These three pillars are inseparable in practice. Parameter design without orchestration may create guardrails but fail to govern how actions unfold in real workflows. Orchestration without telemetry may produce elegant pathways that degrade silently without detection. Telemetry without disciplined parameter design may create visibility into a system that was never adequately bounded in the first place. Architectural leadership demands all three because intelligent systems fail not only through flawed models, but through weak boundaries, careless pathways, and invisible drift.

The architect-leader understands this. The work of leadership is no longer limited to inspiring teams or reviewing deliverables after the fact. It now includes designing the conditions under which intelligent systems can operate with discipline, create value with legitimacy, and remain aligned with mission even as complexity increases. These pillars form the structural core of that responsibility.

The Death of the Review and the Birth of the Audit

In a human centered enterprise, one of the defining rituals of management is, the performance review. The review looks backward. It evaluates results, behaviors, and outcomes over a given period. A manager considers whether goals were met, whether quality standards were achieved, whether development has occurred, and whether intervention is needed. The underlying assumption is clear: work is performed by people, and when something goes wrong, the primary task is to evaluate the individual or team responsible for the result.

That logic begins to break down in a system centered organization.

When intelligent systems are embedded into core workflow, errors cannot be understood adequately through the language of individual performance alone. A flawed output generated by an intelligent assistant, an unauthorized recommendation surfaced by a model driven process, or a compliance failure triggered by an automated workflow is rarely the result of a single isolated malfunction. It is usually the product of interacting architectural conditions. The issue may reside in the prompt design, in the retrieval layer, in corrupted or incomplete source data, in poorly governed integrations, in weak authentication, in missing approval thresholds, in broken exception handling, or in the workflow logic that converted a questionable output into real action. In other words, when a system fails, the failure is seldom a glitch in a vacuum. It is more often a symptom of a deeper architectural weakness.

This changes the posture of leadership. In place of the traditional review, the architect-leader must adopt the discipline of the systemic audit.

The distinction is critical. A review asks whether the visible result was satisfactory. An audit asks how the result became possible. A review tends to focus on the immediate product. An audit traces the chain of causes, dependencies, permissions, and controls that produced the outcome. A review may conclude that an error occurred. An audit seeks to determine whether the error was structurally inevitable under the existing design. This is a far more powerful form of inquiry because it treats failure not as an isolated embarrassment, but as evidence about the health of the system itself.

Consider a system that generates inaccurate or noncompliant guidance. A superficial review might focus on the output and ask whether the content should have been caught before release. A systemic audit asks more fundamental questions.

Did the prompt structure encourage overconfident synthesis. Did the retrieval augmented generation layer draw from stale or contaminated data. Were source documents ranked correctly. Did access permissions expose sensitive material to the model. Were confidence thresholds too low for autonomous release. Did the workflow fail to require human review in a context where judgment remained essential. Was the API exchange protected appropriately. Were logs preserved in sufficient detail to reconstruct the event. Each of these questions shifts attention away from blaming the machine as though it were an unpredictable actor and toward examining the architecture that allowed the failure to occur.

This is one of the most important mental transitions in the entire book. When leaders stop treating system errors as mysterious acts of technological misbehavior and start treating them as design signals, they gain leverage. They move from frustration to diagnosis. They move from passively enduring complexity to actively governing it. They stop asking why the machine betrayed them and start asking what structural assumption, missing control, or design flaw made the failure foreseeable. In that transition, leadership matures.

The audit, then, is not merely a compliance exercise or a post incident ritual. It is a core operating practice of intelligent system governance. It is how leaders validate whether the system remains aligned with mission, whether controls are functioning as intended, whether autonomy is bounded appropriately, and whether observed outcomes are consistent with the logic the organization believes it has established. The audit is not limited to detecting errors. It is how institutions learn. It allows them to identify patterns, correct weak design choices, refine workflows, strengthen telemetry, and recalibrate their risk posture in light of lived operational evidence.

There is also an important cultural implication here. In human organizations, constant review can sometimes devolve into blame, defensiveness, or performative compliance. In system centered organizations, the audit can become something more constructive if it is led well. It can become a disciplined mechanism for collective learning about architecture. It can reinforce the idea that responsibility lies not in scapegoating a single output or a single technical team, but in understanding the broader design environment that shaped behavior. That shift helps institutions become more resilient because it directs attention toward causes rather than appearances.

This is not to say that human accountability disappears. On the contrary, accountability deepens. Leaders, architects, engineers, policy owners, and governance teams each hold responsibility for different aspects of the system's behavior. But that accountability is no longer exercised only through individual assessment. It is exercised through architectural examination. The question is not only who approved the output. The question is who designed the conditions under which the output could be generated, trusted, and operationalized. That is a more demanding standard, but it is also a more honest one.

When leaders embrace the logic of the audit, they begin to reclaim authority over technology rather than merely reacting to it. They cease to be victims of system complexity. They become students of structure, interpreters of failure, and governors of design. This is what true mastery looks like in the age of intelligent systems. Power no longer comes from standing above the machine in abstract authority. It comes from understanding how the architecture works, where it bends, where it breaks, and how it can be rebuilt with greater discipline.

The performance review belonged to an era in which value was produced primarily through visible human effort. The systemic audit belongs to an era in which value increasingly emerges from the interaction of people, logic, workflows, and controls. The review asked whether the work was done well. The audit asks whether the system itself deserves to be trusted. For the architect-leader, that is now the more important question.

The Clarity of Intent

Among the many risks facing the architect-leader, few are more dangerous than ambiguity. In traditional organizations, ambiguity often survives longer than it should. Teams compensate for vague direction through informal norms, intuition, experience, hallway conversations, and a shared sense of what leadership probably meant. Human systems are imperfect, but they are often remarkably adaptive. People can infer priorities from tone, interpret partial signals, reconcile contradictions, and fill in gaps left by weak communication. Entire organizations have operated for years on unwritten assumptions and still managed to function, if not always efficiently, at least recognizably.

Intelligent systems do not operate that way.

Machines do not interpret intention through atmosphere, social cues, or institutional mood. They do not understand strategic drift disguised as flexibility. They do not reliably reconcile conflicting objectives unless those conflicts have been anticipated and structured into the system. They are literal where organizations are often informal. They are procedural where human teams are often interpretive. For that reason, ambiguity that might be manageable in a purely human environment becomes far more dangerous when translated into automated logic, workflow rules, and machine mediated decisions.

This is why clarity of intent becomes one of the highest forms of leadership in the age of intelligent systems. The architect-leader must know not only what the organization wants to achieve, but also how to express that objective with enough precision that it can be translated into design, policy, workflow, and system behavior. Intent must move from aspiration to structure. It must be defined in terms that can be operationalized, governed, monitored, and audited. A vague strategy may still inspire a room. It cannot reliably govern a machine.

This requirement exposes a deeper truth about executive leadership. Many strategies sound compelling in presentation form yet remain structurally weak when tested for operational translation. They rely on broad language, symbolic commitments, and directional statements that are persuasive to people but unusable in systems. Phrases such as improve customer trust, increase resilience, reduce compliance risk, or innovate responsibly may express worthy ambitions, but unless they are converted into workflows, thresholds, permissions, escalation paths, metrics, and decision criteria, they remain too abstract to govern intelligent behavior. In a system driven environment, unstructured aspiration is not leadership. It is unfinished thinking.

The architect-leader therefore treats clarity not as a communication preference, but as a governing discipline. The question is no longer whether a strategy sounds compelling at the executive's retreat. The question is whether it can survive translation into the architecture of the enterprise. Can it be expressed clearly enough to shape parameters. Can it inform data selection. Can it define acceptable and unacceptable actions. Can it guide workflow design. Can it establish when a system should escalate to human review. Can it be measured after deployment in a way that reveals whether intent and behavior remain aligned. These are the tests that separate rhetorical strategy from executable leadership.

Clarity of intent also protects the institution from a subtler danger: the unintended delegation of judgment. When leaders fail to define objectives precisely, the system still has to act somehow. Gaps in clarity are then filled by default settings, inherited workflow assumptions, vendor logic, undocumented team conventions, or the silent biases embedded into data and process design. In effect, where leadership is imprecise, the system improvises on behalf of the institution. That is a profound surrender of authority, often occurring without anyone formally acknowledging it.

For this reason, clarity is not a luxury in 2026 and beyond. It is a condition of responsible governance. The architect-leader must be able to articulate strategic intent with enough rigor that machines can be directed without distorting mission. This does not mean reducing leadership to mechanistic instruction. It means ensuring that institutional purpose is expressed with sufficient discipline to survive contact with automation. The leader must be able to say, with precision, what the system is for, what it is not for, what it may decide, what it may recommend, what it must escalate, what risks are tolerable, and what principles remain nonnegotiable.

This may be the ultimate leadership test of the intelligent systems era. Can the executive articulate strategy clearly enough that it can be translated into machine governed action without losing its ethical core, operational coherence, or institutional intent? If the answer is no, then the system will not truly be led. It will merely be deployed. And deployment without leadership is simply a faster route to drift.

The architect-leader understands that clarity is not the opposite of complexity. It is the discipline that makes complexity governable. In a world increasingly shaped by intelligent systems, the leader who cannot define intent with precision will eventually discover that someone, or something else has defined it for them.

Conclusion: The New Mandate

The rise of the architect-leader signals more than a shift in management style. It marks a redefinition of executive responsibility for the age of intelligent systems. To lead well in this environment does not require the mastery of every programming language, the ability to write every line of code, or the technical depth to engineer every component personally. That has never been the true standard of leadership. The real standard is more demanding in a different way. It is the ability to understand how the pieces fit together, how they interact under pressure, where risk accumulates, where control must be exercised, and how the architecture of the enterprise can be designed to protect mission, trust, and institutional continuity.

This is why the metaphor of the policeman's badge must give way to the architect's blueprint. The older leadership model emphasized supervision, correction, and enforcement after the fact. It assumed that the primary challenge was keeping people aligned with expectations once work was already underway. The emerging model places greater emphasis on design, structure, and precondition. It assumes that in high velocity, machine mediated environments, the most decisive act of leadership often occurs before the workflow begins. The leader must shape the architecture within which decisions will be made, actions will be taken, and consequences will unfold.

That is the new mandate. The architect-leader must define guardrails before autonomy is scaled. The architect-leader must govern logic before outputs proliferate. The architect-leader must insist on telemetry before drift becomes invisible. The architect-leader must translate strategy into workflows, workflows into controls, and controls into trust. Most of all, the architect-leader must remain accountable for the fact that delegated agency, once embedded into systems, does not reduce the burden of leadership. It intensifies it.

Yet this transformation also introduces a new tension. The intelligent enterprise is built for speed. It promises faster decisions, faster workflows, faster adaptation, and faster execution at scales human institutions alone could never sustain. But speed creates its own form of danger when it outruns legitimacy. An organization may automate brilliantly and still erode the very trust on which its long-term viability depends. It may move quickly and still compromise judgment. It may scale intelligence and still weaken confidence if customers, employees, regulators, and stakeholders begin to suspect that the system is no longer understandable, fair, or accountable.

This is the unresolved challenge standing just beyond the architect-leader's blueprint. How can institutions move with velocity without breaking the trust they are meant to preserve? How can they accelerate intelligently without sacrificing coherence, accountability, and human confidence in the process? These questions lead directly into the next chapter, because trust is not peripheral to the intelligent enterprise. It is its fuel.

The next chapter will explore that reality in depth through one of the defining concepts of leadership in this era: the velocity of trust.

3: The Velocity of Trust

The Great Misconception: Governance as a Brake

In nearly every modern enterprise, an unspoken tension exists between two institutional instincts. On one side are the innovators: leaders eager to deploy agentic workflows, automate customer interactions, accelerate decision cycles, and scale operations at the speed of connected systems. On the other side are the governors: the professionals in governance, risk, compliance, legal, and security functions who are often perceived as cautious, procedural, and resistant to momentum. In many boardrooms, these two groups are framed as opposing forces. Innovation is treated as motion. Governance is treated as drag. One side is expected to build the future, while the other is expected to slow it down.

That framing is not only simplistic. It is strategically dangerous.

The belief that governance exists primarily to restrain speed reflects a fundamental misunderstanding of how speed actually works in complex systems. In highly interconnected environments, the ability to move quickly does not come from the absence of controls. It comes from confidence in the controls that are present. Speed is sustainable only when leaders know that failure can be contained, anomalies can be detected, interventions can occur in time, and the consequences of error will not cascade beyond what the institution can absorb. Where such confidence is absent, apparent freedom quickly becomes fragile.

A simple analogy makes the point clear. In a car, brakes do not exist to prevent motion. They exist to make high speed possible. No rational driver would accelerate with confidence in a vehicle that lacked a functioning braking system. Without brakes, every increase in speed multiplies fear because the ability to recover has been removed. The presence of reliable brakes changes the psychology of motion. It gives the driver confidence that acceleration can be matched by control, that hazards can be managed, and that velocity need not become reckless. Breaks are not the enemy of speed. They are the conditions that makes speed survivable.

The same is true in the age of intelligent systems. Governance is the braking system of the modern enterprise. It is what allows leaders to authorize speed without surrendering judgment. It creates the confidence necessary to automate workflows, deploy model driven capabilities, and scale machine mediated decisions beyond the limits of direct human supervision. Without governance, organizations are not truly fast. They are merely exposed. In the absence of reliable controls, every new deployment carries unbounded risk: a compliance failure that spreads before detection, a data leak triggered by poorly constrained access, an insecure integration that compromises downstream systems, a biased recommendation that becomes public, or an automated process that operates beyond the institution's ethical and legal tolerance. Under such conditions, the organization cannot move with confidence. It must either slow itself to a crawl or accept a level of risk that no serious leader should tolerate.

This is why the opposition between innovators and governors is so often misguided. The most mature institutions do not treat governance and innovation as enemies. They understand them as interdependent capabilities. Innovation expands what the enterprise can do. Governance determines what the enterprise can do safely, repeatably, and at scale. Innovation creates motion. Governance makes motion trustworthy. Innovation without governance may create impressive demonstrations, but it rarely produces durable institutional advantage. Governance without innovation may preserve stability, but at the cost of adaptation and relevance. The real challenge of leadership is not to choose between them. It is to integrate them so completely that control and speed reinforce one another.

In intelligent enterprises, that integration becomes even more essential because automation compresses the time available for correction. A flawed manual process may fail slowly enough for human judgment to catch it. A flawed autonomous process can propagate error at machine speed across customers, systems, records, and decisions before anyone realizes what has happened. The faster the system, the more dangerous ungoverned movement becomes. For that reason, governance is not a secondary concern to be layered on after deployment. It must be designed into the architecture from the beginning. It must exist in the parameters, the approvals, the escalation pathways, the audit trails, the access controls, the exception handling logic, and the kill switches that allow the institution to preserve authority even under conditions of high velocity.

This is the first great lesson of trust in the intelligent enterprise. What appears to slow an organization in the short term often becomes the very capability that allows it to move faster over time. Teams that do not trust the control environment hesitate, duplicate reviews, layer on manual checks, and delay release decisions because uncertainty remains too high. Teams that trust the system's guardrails are able to move with greater confidence because they know how the institution will respond when conditions deviate from expectation. In that sense, governance is not merely a protective function. It is an enabling function. It converts anxiety into controlled acceleration.

The mature leader therefore stops asking whether governance will reduce speed and begins asking a more sophisticated question: what kind of governance architecture is necessary to produce trustworthy speed? That question reframes the entire conversation. It recognizes that velocity in intelligent systems is never just a function of computational capability. It is a function of confidence. And confidence, when properly earned, is built on governance.

Trust as a Technical Variable

In ordinary conversation, trust is often treated as a soft concept. It is associated with character, interpersonal reliability, institutional reputation, and the confidence that develops between people over time. In many leadership settings, trust is discussed as a cultural asset, a matter of communication, credibility, and consistency of human behavior. All that remains important. But in the architecture of intelligent systems, trust must be understood in a more operational way. It cannot remain only a feeling. It must become a measurable condition.

This is one of the most important conceptual shifts in the intelligent enterprise. When decisions, recommendations, and actions are increasingly mediated by systems, trust can no longer be left undefined. Leaders must be able to assess whether a given system deserves confidence, whether a workflow can be allowed to operate at speed, and whether intervention is likely to occur in time when conditions begin to drift. In that context, trust becomes a technical variable. It is not merely something an organization hopes to have. It is something it must be able to evaluate, design for, and improve.

A useful way to express this is through a simple but powerful formula:

Trust = (Visibility + Consistency) / Latency

The strength of this model lies in its clarity. It reframes trust not as sentiment, but as a function of three governing conditions: visibility, consistency, and latency. Together, these variables help explain why some organizations move with extraordinary confidence while others remain trapped in hesitation, rework, and manual oversight even when they possess advanced technical tools.

The first variable is *visibility*. Visibility asks a basic but decisive question: can leaders and operators see what the system is doing in real time, with enough detail to understand its behavior, track its decisions, and detect emerging problems before they become institutional failures? Visibility includes telemetry, observability, workflow status, audit logging, control validation, and the ability to trace actions across the system lifecycle. A system that cannot be seen clearly cannot be trusted deeply. Leaders may admire its output when conditions are favorable, but they will hesitate to scale it because they lack confidence in their ability to govern it under stress. Visibility reduces uncertainty by making system behavior legible. It turns opaque automation into something that can be monitored, interpreted, and, when necessary, challenged.

The second variable is *consistency*. Consistency asks whether the system produces reliable, high quality, policy aligned outcomes when the relevant conditions are met. A system may perform brilliantly in isolated moments and still be untrustworthy if its behavior varies unpredictably from one situation to the next. Consistency is what allows institutions to develop operational confidence. It is the evidence that the system is not merely capable, but dependable. In practical terms, consistency means that comparable inputs, governed by the same parameters and subject to the same policies, should produce outputs that remain stable enough to support executive reliance. It also means that quality and compliance are not occasional successes, but repeatable characteristics of the system's operation. Without consistency, every output becomes a fresh negotiation. With consistency, oversight can become more strategic because the organization no longer needs to revalidate the entire system at every step.

The third variable is *latency*. Latency, in this framework, is not merely a technical measure of system response time. It is a leadership measure of delay between system action and human understanding or intervention. How long does it take for a leader, operator, reviewer, or control owner to verify a decision, detect an anomaly, halt a workflow, or redirect a process that is moving off course? High latency is toxic to trust because it means the organization cannot respond at the speed of the system it has deployed. A workflow may appear efficient on paper, but if intervention requires slow manual investigation, fragmented reporting, or delayed escalation, then the institution is functionally operating without timely control. Low latency, by contrast, means that leaders retain practical authority. They can see, decide, and intervene before the system's velocity outruns governance.

Taken together, these variables reveal a powerful principle. Trust rises when visibility is high, consistency is strong, and latency is low. In such an environment, leaders gain confidence not because they believe the system is perfect, but because they know it is observable, dependable, and governable at the speed at which it operates. Conversely, trust deteriorates when the system is opaque, erratic, or too fast for meaningful human oversight. Under those conditions, the institution instinctively compensates by slowing down. It adds manual checks, demands repeated approvals, inserts redundant reviews, and reduces autonomy because trust has not been earned structurally.

This insight helps explain why some organizations, despite possessing advanced models and substantial digital investment, never achieve systemic velocity. The issue is not always a lack of technical capability. More often, it is a lack of technical trust. They cannot move quickly because they do not know what the system is doing, cannot predict what it will do next, or cannot intervene before consequences propagate. As a result, the organization becomes dependent on friction for safety. Manual oversight becomes a substitute for architectural confidence.

The most mature enterprises take the opposite path. They treat trust as an engineering and governance objective. They invest in telemetry to improve visibility. They refine controls, data quality, and workflow design to improve consistency. They reduce approval bottlenecks, improve escalation logic, and streamline decision pathways to reduce latency. In doing so, they do not merely make the system more efficient. They make it more trustworthy. And trust, once established on technical and governance foundations, becomes the fuel of systemic velocity.

That is the deeper meaning of the formula. Trust is not peripheral to speed. It is what makes speed legitimate. An organization that cannot calculate, strengthen, and defend the trustworthiness of its intelligent systems will never move as fast as its technical architecture suggests it should. It will remain constrained by caution because caution is what institutions naturally produce when trust is missing. But when visibility is clear, consistency is proven, and latency is low, trust ceases to be an abstract aspiration. It becomes a strategic asset.

And in the intelligent enterprise, strategic assets are what determine velocity.

The Cost of Friction: The Manual Verification Trap

If trust is the fuel of velocity, then friction is its greatest enemy. Every intelligent enterprise eventually confronts a difficult reality: the presence of advanced systems does not automatically produce organizational speed. A model may process information in seconds, classify risk at scale, or generate recommendations with extraordinary efficiency, yet the institution surrounding it may still move slowly. The reason is often not technological weakness. It is the persistence of friction embedded in human process.

In many organizations, that friction is unmistakably human shaped. It appears in mandatory reviews, redundant approvals, manual handoffs, serial signoffs, fragmented control ownership, and habitual verification rituals built for an earlier era of work. These practices often emerge from legitimate concerns. Leaders want assurance. Compliance teams want defensibility. Risk owners want evidence that controls were followed. Legal teams want confidence that policy has not been bypassed. None of these motivations are inherently wrong. In fact, many were developed precisely because they reduced exposure in environments where human review was the primary method of maintaining quality and accountability.

The problem arises when those same mechanisms are carried unchanged into systems capable of operating at machine scale. At that point, the organization creates a structural contradiction. It deploys intelligent systems to achieve speed but preserves review models designed for manual work. The result is a false appearance of automation. The machine is fast, but the institution is still slow.

Consider a system capable of processing one thousand vendor risk assessments in an hour. On paper, the organization appears to have made a substantial leap in capability. Intake is accelerated. Analysis is automated. Scoring is immediate. Routing is seamless. Yet if the governance process still requires a human GRC officer to examine and approve every single assessment before action can proceed, the essential bottleneck remains unchanged. The point of delay has merely shifted from the front end of the workflow to the back end. What looks like transformation is often only redistribution of congestion.

This is the manual verification trap.

The trap is dangerous because it creates the illusion of progress while preserving the logic of the old operating model. Leaders see fast systems and assume the organization has become more agile. In reality, they have only intensified pressure on the human control points that remain. Review teams become overwhelmed by volume. Decision latency increases. Backlogs accumulate. Exceptions multiply. The system continues producing outputs, but the enterprise cannot absorb them at the speed they are generated. Over time, one of two things usually happens. Either the organization silently slows the system down to match the review capacity it actually possesses, or reviewers begin approving at a pace too fast for meaningful scrutiny, turning oversight into ritual rather than assurance. Neither outcome represents mature governance.

The deeper issue is architectural. Manual verification assumes that safety is achieved primarily through the fact human inspection. That assumption may work in limited or high consequence cases, but it cannot scale as the default control model for intelligent systems. When every output must be touched by a person before value can be realized, the organization remains structurally dependent on friction for safety. In that model, humans are not governing the system strategically. They serve as throughput constraints.

This is why the architect-leader must make a more disciplined distinction between approval and assurance. Manual approval asks a person to certify each instance of work. Automated assurance asks whether the system itself has been designed so that routine work can proceed safely within bounded, observable, and controlled conditions.

Approval is episodic and labor intensive. Assurance is structural and repeatable. Approval relies on human inspection of individual artifacts. Assurance relies on architecture that embeds policy into the pathway of execution. Approval is often necessary at the edge of uncertainty. Assurance is what allows the center of the workflow to move.

Breaking the manual verification trap does not mean eliminating human judgment. It means reserving human judgment for the places where it adds the most value. Low risk, highly repeatable, well bounded decisions should not require the same oversight model as ambiguous, material, or high consequence actions. The mature enterprise learns to distinguish between the two. It reduces friction where confidence can be earned structurally and concentrates attention where discernment remains essential. That is how institutions move from symbolic automation to real velocity.

The cost of friction is therefore larger than delay alone. Friction consumes expert attention, erodes the benefits of automation, and obscures the difference between activity and progress. It convinces leaders they are scaling when in fact they are only generating more work for the same control structure. True velocity begins only when the organization stops treating manual verification as the universal answer and starts redesigning assurance at the level of architecture.

Refining the Trust Formula: The Mathematical Proof of Speed

If intelligent systems are to operate at enterprise scale, trust cannot remain a metaphor alone. It must be refined into a dynamic operating variable, something leaders can observe, shape, and improve over time. In practical terms, trust is best understood as the managed reduction of uncertainty within a high velocity environment. The more clearly a system can be seen, the more reliably it behaves, and the faster meaningful intervention can occur, the more confidently an institution can allow that system to act. In this sense, trust is not merely adjacent to risk. It is the inverse pressure acting against it. As trust rises, operational uncertainty falls. As uncertainty falls, the institution gains the ability to move with greater speed and less hesitation.

This is why the trust formula introduced earlier deserves refinement. It is not simply a conceptual device for discussing confidence. It is a disciplined framework for understanding the architecture of speed itself. The core relationship remains:

Trust = (Visibility + Consistency) / Latency

At a high level, the equation expresses a straightforward principle. Trust increases when the organization can see what the system is doing, when the system behaves dependably under governed conditions, and when the delay between machine action and human understanding or intervention remains low. Yet the usefulness of the formula becomes clearer when each variable is examined with greater precision.

Visibility, represented here as **V**, refers to the density and quality of real time telemetry available to leadership, operators, and control owners. Visibility is not simply whether logs exist somewhere in the environment. It is the extent to which the decision-making process is exposed in a timely, intelligible, and actionable form through observability platforms, GRC dashboards, workflow monitoring layers, or a clarity portal that renders system behavior visible at the level required for governance. Visibility asks whether leaders can trace how a decision moved, what inputs informed it, what controls were triggered, where exceptions occurred, and how the workflow evolved from inference to action. A system with low visibility may still be technically sophisticated, but it cannot be trusted deeply because its behavior remains partly hidden from those responsible for governing it.

Consistency, represented as **C**, refers to the degree of dependable behavioral alignment under equivalent governed conditions. Put simply, if the system receives the same input **x** under the same conditions **y**, does it reliably produce the same compliant output **z**. This does not mean that every intelligent system must be perfectly deterministic in the mathematical sense. Many advanced systems include probabilistic behaviors. The question for leadership is not absolute sameness in every microscopic detail, but dependable sameness in the dimensions that matter institutionally. Does the system remain policy aligned. Does it honor thresholds. Does it apply rules reliably. Does it preserve quality and compliance under repeatable conditions. Consistency is what allows the institution to move from cautious experimentation to justified reliance. Without it, every output remains a fresh uncertainty.

Latency, represented as **L**, captures the temporal drag between system action and meaningful human verification, interpretation, or intervention. In many enterprises, latency is the hidden variable that quietly destroys velocity while leaving the technical architecture looking impressive on paper. A system may act in seconds, yet if meaningful review requires hours of manual triage, fragmented reporting, or delayed escalation, then the organization is not truly operating at system speed. It is operating at the speed of its slowest control point. Latency therefore measures more than delay. It measures the degree to which human authority remains practically connected to automated behavior. The higher the latency, the weaker the institution's real time control. The lower the latency, the more effective leadership can preserve authority without smothering speed.

Once these variables are defined more carefully, a deeper challenge becomes visible. They do not always move in harmony. In fact, they frequently conflict.

This is one of the central tensions the architect-leader must learn to manage. Increasing visibility often produces more data, more signals, more dashboards, more logs, and more events requiring interpretation. If visibility expands without corresponding discipline, latency may rise rather than fall because human operators become flooded by information they cannot prioritize effectively. The result is a familiar failure mode: analysis paralysis. The organization gains more data but loses decision velocity because the telemetry environment is too noisy to support timely judgment. In such cases, visibility has increased in quantity without increasing in governance value.

That is why the clarity mindset is so important. The objective is not simply to maximize raw visibility. The objective is to maximize meaningful visibility while minimizing unnecessary latency through automated assurance. Leaders do not need every possible signal elevated to the level of executive attention. They need governed telemetry that identifies the conditions that matter, surfaces anomalies rather than routine activity, and allows intervention to occur where the system is truly drifting from expected behavior. In other words, visibility must be curated, not merely accumulated.

The formula therefore teaches a discipline of balance. Trust is strengthened not by collecting endless information, but by designing an environment in which visibility is relevant, consistency is proven, and latency is compressed through architecture rather than brute force human effort. When those conditions hold, speed ceases to be reckless acceleration and becomes governed motion. The equation is not merely descriptive. It is, in effect, a mathematical proof of why some institutions can move faster than others without sacrificing control. They have learned how to transform trust from a cultural abstraction into an engineered condition of enterprise performance.

Automation via Assurance: The GRC Flywheel

The path out of the manual verification trap is not reckless automation. It is disciplined assurance. Intelligent enterprises do not achieve velocity by removing governance. They achieve velocity by moving governance into the architecture of the workflow itself. This is the crucial distinction. When governance is external to execution, it introduces delay because work must stop and wait to be inspected. When governance is embedded inside execution, control becomes part of how the work moves. The system no longer needs to be checked at the end of every task because the workflow has already been designed to prevent unauthorized, unsafe, or noncompliant action from proceeding unchecked.

This is the operating principle behind automated assurance.

Automated assurance begins with a simple but powerful design philosophy: instead of asking whether work should be reviewed after it is completed, the organization asks how the workflow can be structured so that work cannot be completed unless the right conditions are met. In this model, governance is no longer a checkpoint added after the fact. It becomes a series of logic gates embedded directly into the path of action. Each gate expresses a policy decision, a control requirement, a risk threshold, or an accountability boundary. The system is permitted to proceed only when those requirements are satisfied.

The implications of this shift are profound. If required privacy conditions are not met, the API does not fire. If the confidence score falls below an established threshold, the output is not released autonomously. If the risk score rises above a defined level, the case is automatically routed to a human reviewer. If a data source fails validation, ingestion is halted before flawed input contaminates downstream action. If an access request violates role policy, the workflow terminates or escalates immediately. In each case, governance is not being applied as a separate review ritual. Governance is functioning as an intrinsic property of execution.

This is where governance, risk, and compliance begin to evolve from a defensive function into an enabling architecture. The controls do not merely constrain behavior. They create the conditions under which behavior can scale safely. They reduce the need for broad manual review because the system itself is already enforcing the institution's rules at the moment action is attempted. Properly designed, these logic gates do not eliminate human involvement. They preserve it for situations that genuinely require interpretation, discretion, or exception handling. Routine work is allowed to flow. Ambiguous work is elevated. High risk work is paused or redirected. The workflow becomes more intelligent not only because the model is capable, but because the control environment is mature.

From this design logic emerges what may be called the *GRC flywheel*. The flywheel begins with a bounded domain of low risk, high repeatability work. The organization embeds governance into the workflow through automated logic gates, clear thresholds, auditable pathways, and well-defined escalation rules. As the system repeatedly demonstrates that it can process these tasks accurately, compliantly, and with low intervention, the institution's trust quotient rises. That increase in trust is not emotional or symbolic. It is earned through observed performance, consistent outcomes, and reduced need for manual correction.

As trust rises, leaders gain the confidence to widen the guardrails selectively. The system may be granted more autonomy in adjacent low risk cases. Thresholds may be recalibrated. Certain human approval steps may be removed because the evidence now shows that the system can be trusted to operate safely within clearly defined bounds. With each cycle, the enterprise gains both velocity and learning. Greater trust enables broader autonomy. Broader autonomy, when properly governed, creates more evidence of dependable performance. That evidence, in turn, supports further expansion. Over time, the organization does not merely automate tasks. It builds a self-reinforcing cycle in which trust, control, and speed strengthen one another.

The power of the flywheel lies in its discipline. It does not assume that autonomy should be granted all at once. It assumes that autonomy should be earned. It does not remove governance to gain speed. It uses governance to make speed sustainable. And it does not treat trust as a vague cultural sentiment. It treats trust as a measurable outcome of system design, workflow integrity, and maturity control.

This is one of the central leadership lessons of the intelligent enterprise. Organizations do not become fast because they are willing to take more risk blindly. They become fast because they have learned how to structure risk intelligently. They know where automation can be trusted, where human judgment must remain in the loop, and how to design the transitions between those states without creating dangerous ambiguity. That is what automated assurance makes possible.

For the architect-leader, the GRC flywheel offers a far more mature model of progress than either endless manual oversight or naive enthusiasm for autonomy. It provides a path for scaling intelligent systems without sacrificing trust. It allows governance to become a source of momentum rather than delay. Most importantly, it gives the enterprise a mechanism for converting disciplined design into durable velocity.

The Primary Casualty: Why Speed Fails

When organizations pursue speed without governance, the first casualty is almost always trust. This pattern repeats so often that it should no longer be treated as an exception. A system is deployed aggressively in the name of innovation, efficiency, or competitive urgency. Early demonstrations look promising. Output is fast. Costs appear lower. Executive enthusiasm rises. Then a failure occurs. The system hallucinates a material financial error, exposes sensitive customer data, misclassifies a compliance obligation, generates a biased outcome, or executes an action outside the organization's ethical or regulatory tolerance. In that moment, the problem is no longer technical alone. It becomes institutional.

Trust, once fractured at that scale, rarely fails in isolation. The damage spreads across multiple layers of the enterprise. Operational teams begin to doubt the dependability of the system. Governance teams become more skeptical of automation broadly. Senior leadership loses confidence in the deployment judgment that authorized the rollout. Boards begin asking whether the organization moved too quickly. External stakeholders question whether innovation was prioritized over responsibility. A single high-profile breakdown can therefore undermine not only confidence in the system itself, but confidence in the leadership model that surrounded it.

This is why trust must be understood as the primary casualty of ungoverned speed. When a failure of this kind occurs, the institution does not merely suffer an isolated incident. It suffers a collapse in permission. The willingness to let the system act declines sharply. The latitude once granted to automated workflows narrows. Approvals return. Manual reviews multiply. Exceptional scrutiny becomes the new default. Even teams that were not directly affected often become more hesitant because the symbolic impact of failure exceeds the immediate operational impact. Trust contracts faster than capability can expand.

The result is what may be called *governance whiplash.*

Governance whiplash occurs when an organization moves too far toward unconstrained automation, experiences a visible or material failure, and then recoils sharply in the opposite direction. The board panics. Executives suspend initiatives. Automation is paused or dismantled. Manual work is reinstated. New approval layers are added. The institution attempts to recover control through friction because it no longer believes the architecture can be trusted. In many cases, this reaction is understandable. But it is also costly. The organization does not simply lose time. It loses confidence, continuity, and often the strategic advantage that intelligent systems were meant to create in the first place.

This pattern should be recognized for what it is: not proof that speed is dangerous in itself, but proof that speed without trust is unstable. Institutions do not fail because they moved quickly. They fail because they moved quickly without building the governance conditions that would have made velocity credible. The collapse that follows is then misread as evidence that automation was the mistake, when the real mistake was architectural immaturity.

For the architect-leader, the lesson is clear. The goal is not to maximize autonomy at the expense of trust, nor to preserve trust by eliminating speed. The goal is to refuse the false choice entirely. Durable speed is speed that can survive scrutiny, error, and intervention without requiring a full institutional retreat. It is speed built on observability, bounded authority, escalation logic, and maturity control. When those foundations are absent, the enterprise remains vulnerable to whiplash because it has confused acceleration with readiness.

Trust, then, is more than a precondition for velocity. It is also the protective layer that prevents isolated failure from becoming strategic regression. Without it, one incident can reverse years of progress. With it, the organization can absorb errors, learn from them, and continue moving. That is the difference between fragile speed and resilient speed. One collapses under pressure. The other matures through it.

Conclusion: Leading at Scale

The purpose of this chapter is not to teach caution as an end in itself. It is to teach a more disciplined kind of fearlessness. True fearlessness in the age of intelligent systems does not come from ignoring risk, minimizing governance, or if technical power will somehow regulate itself. It comes from building an enterprise architecture so grounded in visibility, consistency, and low latency control that leadership can authorize speed without surrendering integrity.

That is the deeper promise of systemic trust. When trust is designed into the architecture, the organization is no longer forced to choose between movement and control. It can scale what once seemed unscalable. It can automate with confidence rather than anxiety. It can move from hoping that the AI will behave responsibly to knowing that the surrounding system has been built to preserve accountability, transparency, and intervention at the speed required by the modern enterprise. In that environment, trust is no longer a vague cultural aspiration. It becomes an operating asset.

This is the threshold of leadership at scale. The architect-leader does not seek speed for its own sake. The architect-leader seeks governed speed, the kind of motion that remains aligned with mission even under pressure. Such leadership requires more than enthusiasm for innovation. It requires discipline to ensure that every increase in capability is matched by an increase in observability, assurance, and structural control. The institution must be able to say not only that it can move fast, but that it can explain how it moves, why it moves, and what mechanisms exist to keep that movement within acceptable bounds.

Yet this raises the next and perhaps more technical question. If trust is the fuel of velocity, then what exactly must be engineered into the enterprise to preserve that trust in real time. How does an organization avoid relying on retrospective checks and instead build the logic of integrity directly into the operating environment. How does it ensure that oversight is not episodic, delayed, or symbolic, but continuous, living, and embedded in the very plumbing of the company.

Those questions carry the discussion from the philosophical foundations of Part I into the engineering demands of Part II. The next step is no longer simply to define trust, but to operationalize it. That journey begins by rethinking one of the most important and often misunderstood functions in the modern enterprise: real time compliance.

Bridging the Chasm: From Theory to Telemetry

Part I has argued for a paradigm shift.

Leadership in the age of intelligent systems can no longer be defined by oversight alone, nor by the inherited assumptions of the traditional management era. The leader of the intelligent enterprise must become something more than a supervisor of outputs or a coordinator of human effort. The leader must become an architect of conditions, a governor of logic, and a steward of trust at machine speed.

Yet even the clearest paradigm is insufficient if it remains only conceptual. In an enterprise setting, an idea without implementation is not transformation. It is aspiration. A leadership philosophy without operational embodiment may inspire, but it cannot govern. A trust framework without systemic enforcement may persuade, but it cannot scale.

That is the chasm now before us: the movement from theory to telemetry.

The velocity of trust will not be achieved through stronger rhetoric, more persuasive slide decks, or better meetings about alignment. It will be achieved through disciplined engineering. It will be achieved when governance is no longer treated as a periodic checkpoint, but as a living layer within the architecture of the enterprise itself. If an organization intends to move at the speed of an API, then its oversight must be built into the API. If it intends to automate decisions at scale, then control must move at the speed of those decisions. If it intends to preserve trust in high velocity environments, then accountability can no longer remain manual, delayed, or retrospective. It must become embedded, continuous, and real time.

This is the turning point of the book.

Part I, **The Paradigm Shift**, has reframed how leadership must think. It has established that artificial intelligence is only one component of a larger intelligent system, that governance is the condition of trustworthy speed, and that the modern executive must evolve into an architect-leader capable of designing for resilience, visibility, and control. Those ideas form the intellectual foundation of the intelligent enterprise.

Part II, **Engineering the Governance Layer**, turns from rethinking to rebuilding.

The question is no longer only what leaders must understand. The question is how understanding becomes implementation. How are trust, accountability, and oversight translated into workflows, logic gates, telemetry, and operating controls. How does an organization move from philosophical agreement to technical enforcement. How does leadership become visible in the actual machinery of decision making.

To answer those questions, we must enter the engine room of the enterprise.

We begin where the old model of governance is already failing: with the end of the snapshot audit and the birth of real time compliance.

Case Study: The Cost of the Trust Deficit

To understand why the trust formula matters in practice, consider a representative failure pattern that emerged in 2024 within a major aerospace supply chain automation environment. The details here are best read not merely as an isolated incident, but as a revealing example of what happens when intelligent systems are deployed into an architecture that has not yet earned the trust required for high velocity operation.

The organization in question, a Tier 1 defense contractor, implemented an intelligent agent to manage sub vendor compliance across a fast-moving supplier ecosystem. The objective was straightforward and strategically sound. The company needed to accelerate procurement workflows while maintaining rigorous security and compliance standards across a complex vendor base. To accomplish this, leadership authorized the deployment of an intelligent system designed to evaluate vendor submissions against established security criteria and automatically approve those vendors meeting 98 percent of required controls. On paper, the design promised both speed and scale. Routine compliance work would be automated, procurement velocity would improve, and human experts could reserve their attention for the most consequential exceptions.

At first glance, the system appeared successful. Its consistency was high. For the overwhelming majority of routine cases, the agent produced stable and predictable results. Vendors that met the defined control thresholds were processed quickly, and the organization saw early gains in throughput. Yet beneath that apparent success, a structural weakness was already forming. Visibility into the remaining 2 percent of exceptions was too low. The reasoning behind those edge cases existed, but it was buried inside unstructured logs and fragmented technical artifacts that were not easily surfaced through leadership dashboards or operational workflow views. In effect, the organization had built a system capable of making judgments but had not built a sufficiently clear window into why the most sensitive judgments were being made.

That gap had predictable consequences. Because leadership did not trust the system's handling of the exception cases, it inserted a manual review requirement for all exceptions. This seemed prudent. On the surface, human oversight appeared to compensate for the lack of system transparency. In reality, it introduced a high latency control model into a workflow designed for machine speed. The architecture now contained a hidden contradiction. The system could identify and sort cases quickly, but the organization could not resolve ambiguous cases with equivalent speed because trust had not been built into the telemetry environment. The result was a widening queue of items awaiting human validation.

The strain became acute during a procurement surge. Vendor volume increased, pressure mounted, and the manual review queue began to back up beyond the review team's practical capacity. Faced with operational urgency and an expanding bottleneck, a junior analyst took the step that fragile systems often invite under pressure: bulk approval. In an effort to clear the queue and restore flow, the analyst approved fifty vendors at once, effectively bypassing the careful scrutiny that the manual exception process had been intended to provide. One of those vendors carried a compromised TCP session security protocol, which later enabled a lateral movement attack that bypassed the enterprise's Nginx gateway and introduced material downstream exposure.

The post incident response followed a familiar pattern. Leadership's first instinct was to blame the artificial intelligence system. The narrative was emotionally satisfying because it localized failure in the technology itself. Yet a more disciplined analysis reveals a different truth. The primary failure was not the existence of intelligent automation. The primary failure was architectural. The trust quotient of the system was too low to support the operational velocity the business demanded. Visibility into exceptions was insufficient. Consistency in routine cases was not enough to compensate for weak transparency at the edges. Latency was then increased through manual review, creating a pressure buildup inside the workflow. Under that pressure, human behavior became the point of failure. The resulting incident was not evidence that the system moved too fast. It was evidence that the institution tried to force high speed automation into a high latency oversight model that could not absorb the load.

This is the deeper lesson. Trust cannot be bolted onto an intelligent system after deployment. It cannot be manufactured reactively through improvised review queues once the workflow is already moving. Trust must be architected into the telemetry, the visibility model, the escalation pathways, and the exception handling logic from the beginning. When organizations neglect that work, they often create exactly the kind of environment in which human workarounds become more dangerous than the automation they were meant to supervise.

The case also exposes a difficult but important truth about hybrid human machine systems. In fragile architectures, low trust does not produce caution so much as distorted compensation. Leaders respond to low visibility by adding manual oversight. Manual oversight introduces latency. Latency creates backlog. Backlog creates pressure. Pressure invites shortcuts. Shortcuts erode the very control the manual layer was meant to restore. What appears to be a prudent control response can therefore become the mechanism through which risk actually enters the system. This is the pressure cooker effect of the trust deficit.

For the architect-leader, the implication is unmistakable. The objective is not merely to install intelligent systems that perform well under normal conditions. The objective is to build an operating environment in which trust is structurally sufficient to support the required pace of the enterprise. Where trust is weak, velocity becomes brittle. Where trust is strong, speed becomes governable.

The Clarity Threshold

For the architect-leader, one of the most important strategic goals is reaching what may be called the *clarity threshold.* This is the point at which visibility and consistency have become strong enough, and latency has been reduced sufficiently, that standard operations no longer depend on routine human verification to remain safe and compliant. At this threshold, the organization has not eliminated oversight. It has matured oversight to the point that oversight is embedded into the system rather than imposed as a constant external interruption.

Conceptually, the clarity threshold is reached when **V** and **C** are high enough that **L** can be reduced to near zero for ordinary, well bounded, low ambiguity operations. Visibility is high because the system's behavior is exposed through relevant, intelligible, and actionable telemetry. Consistency is high because the workflow produces dependable, policy aligned outcomes under governed conditions. Latency is low because intervention is reserved for meaningful anomalies rather than routine activity. Once these conditions are present together, human review no longer serves as the default mechanism of trust. It becomes the exception mechanism for cases that genuinely require judgment.

This is the practical ambition behind autonomous compliance. The phrase should not be misunderstood as a call for careless automation or the removal of accountability. Properly understood, autonomous compliance means that the workflow itself has been designed so well that compliance is not something checked after the fact for ordinary cases. It is something continuously enforced by the logic of the system as work moves. The organization does not need to rely on constant manual verification because policy thresholds, routing rules, confidence bounds, escalation triggers, and audit trails are already built into execution.

Reaching this threshold is often described as the holy grail of governance, risk, and compliance because it marks a fundamental shift in operating posture. Before the threshold is reached, the institution remains constrained by the speed of human review. No matter how advanced the system appears, the practical pace of the enterprise is limited by how fast people can inspect, validate, and approve what the system produces. After the threshold is reached, the institution is limited far less by manual review capacity and far more by the speed, quality, and discipline of its own logic architecture. That is a profound competitive and operational advantage.

Yet the clarity threshold should never be treated as a destination reached once and then assumed permanently. It is a living condition that must be maintained. Visibility can degrade as systems become more complex. Consistency can weaken as data changes, models drift, or workflows evolve. Latency can creep back in when organizations respond to new risk by adding unstructured approvals instead of refining system assurance. For that reason, the threshold must be monitored continuously. It is less like a finish line and more like a governance equilibrium that requires ongoing stewardship.

What makes the clarity threshold so powerful is that it changes the nature of leadership itself. The leader no longer spends the majority of time deciding whether to trust each individual output. Instead, the leader governs whether the architecture continues to deserve trust. The question moves from isolated approval to systemic integrity. That is the moment when an institution begins to operate as a truly intelligent enterprise.

And that, ultimately, is the promise of the velocity of trust. When clarity is high enough, consistency strong enough, and latency low enough, the organization is no longer trapped in a cycle of hesitation, backlog, and manual correction. It can move at the speed of its logic without abandoning accountability. It can scale without surrendering oversight. It can automate without dissolving trust.

That is not merely operational maturity. It is strategic power.

Part II: Engineering the Governance Layer

The GRC Core

4: Real-Time Compliance

The Death of the Snapshot Audit

For decades, the annual audit stood as one of the defining rituals of corporate integrity. It signaled seriousness, discipline, and accountability. External consultants arrived, documentation was assembled, samples were reviewed, controls were tested, and a formal report was issued that purported to represent the organization's compliance posture. In an earlier era, this model made practical sense. Business processes moved more slowly, transactional complexity was lower, and the gap between operational reality and audit review, while imperfect, was still manageable. A periodic examination could provide at least a reasonable approximation of institutional health.

That world no longer exists.

In the age of intelligent systems, compliance can no longer be governed through delayed observation alone. Enterprises now operate in environments where autonomous workflows, machine assisted decisions, API driven transactions, and constantly shifting data states move at a speed that far exceeds the cadence of traditional assurance models. Systems can execute millions of actions in the span of a single hour. Access rights can change in seconds. Sensitive data can move across environments instantly. Model outputs can be generated, consumed, and operationalized long before a human reviewer has even opened a dashboard. Under such conditions, the old audit model begins to reveal its limitations with unusual clarity.

The problem is not merely that the traditional audit is slow. The problem is that it is structurally retrospective. It looks backward at a slice of activity that has already passed. It offers a point in time representation of control effectiveness based on partial evidence, sampled transactions, interviews, screenshots, attestations, and artifacts collected after the fact. Even when done rigorously, it remains a reconstruction of yesterday's reality. By the time the report is assembled, reviewed, finalized, and distributed, the organization has already changed. New workflows have been deployed. New integrations have been introduced. New exceptions have emerged. New risks have accumulated. The institution is no longer in the state the audit was meant to describe.

This is why the snapshot audit has become more than insufficient. In many contexts, it has become a liability.

A compliance model that depends on periodic retrospective assessment cannot reliably govern systems operating at machine speed. To rely on an annual or quarterly audit as the primary oversight mechanism for autonomous or semi-autonomous systems is to confuse documentation with control. It is like attempting to monitor a Formula 1 race by studying a photograph taken at the starting line. The image may be accurate in the narrowest possible sense, but it tells the observer nothing about what has happened since, what is happening now, or what is about to go wrong in the next turn. The faster the system moves, the more dangerous that gap becomes.

In traditional environments, retrospective audits at least had the virtue of tolerable delay. In intelligent environments, delay itself becomes a governance weakness. A control failure that is visible only after the reporting cycle may have already created regulatory exposure, financial loss, operational disruption, reputational damage, or a systemic trust breakdown before anyone formally recognizes it. The institution is then forced into remediation mode, not because it lacked policy, but because its oversight model was too slow to preserve authority in real time.

The executive implication is profound. Compliance can no longer be understood as an episodic assessment function. It must become a living operational discipline. The central question is no longer whether the organization can prove, after the fact, that it was compliant at a prior moment. The question is whether the enterprise can know, now, whether its systems are operating within acceptable policy, legal, ethical, and risk boundaries as activity unfolds.

That shift marks the death of the snapshot audit.

The Shift to Continuous Control Monitoring

The fall of the snapshot model does not mean the end of assurance. It means the redesign of assurance around a fundamentally different operating reality. In the intelligent enterprise, real-time compliance replaces the isolated audit event with *continuous control monitoring*, often referred to as CCM. This is more than a technical enhancement to the old model. It is a conceptual transformation in how oversight is understood.

Continuous control monitoring moves compliance from historical reporting to live operational awareness. Instead of waiting for a quarter to close or an audit cycle to begin, the organization instruments its environment so that control effectiveness can be observed continuously, exceptions can be identified as they arise, and noncompliant conditions can be detected before they mature into institutional failure. In this model, compliance is no longer something the organization discovers periodically. It becomes something the organization observes, tests, and enforces as part of its daily operating rhythm.

The change can be captured in a single contrast. Legacy governance asks, **Were we compliant last quarter?** Modern governance asks, **Are we compliant right now?** That difference may sound simple, but it reshapes the entire philosophy of oversight. The first question is retrospective and evidentiary. The second is operational and preventive. The first seeks to explain what happened. The second seeks to govern what is happening.

This is why continuous control monitoring matters so much in the age of intelligent systems. When workflows move at machine speed, compliance must move with them. If policy enforcement is delayed until after execution, then the institution has already lost its most meaningful point of control. Real time compliance restores that control by embedding observability, rule validation, threshold detection, exception handling, and escalation logic into the living environment of the system itself.

A useful way to understand the shift is across four dimensions: cadence, data source, response model, and visibility.

Under the *legacy snapshot model*, the cadence of governance is periodic. Reviews occur annually, quarterly, or at other set intervals. The institution lives between examinations, hoping that the control environment remains stable enough for retrospective review to remain meaningful. Under *continuous control monitoring*, the cadence becomes persistent. Oversight is event driven and real time. The system does not wait for a calendar event to ask whether control conditions are intact. It evaluates compliance continuously as activity unfolds.

The *data source* also changes fundamentally. Legacy GRC often depends on manual samples, self-reporting, interviews, spreadsheets, screenshots, and human assembled evidence packages. These artifacts may still have value, but they are indirect and often incomplete. Continuous monitoring draws instead from direct telemetry, system logs, workflow data, access events, configuration states, API calls, and other machine generated evidence streams. In other words, the control environment begins to speak for itself.

The *response model* shifts as well. Legacy compliance is primarily reactive. It identifies gaps after the fact and then initiates remediation, documentation, and corrective action. Continuous control monitoring is proactive. It is designed not merely to discover failure, but to prevent it. It enables automated policy checks, real time alerts, dynamic escalations, and, where appropriate, kill switches that stop a workflow before a breach, violation, or unauthorized action can propagate.

Finally, *visibility* is transformed. Snapshot governance offers what might be called a flashlight view of compliance. It provides narrow, delayed illumination into selected areas of a much larger environment. Continuous monitoring offers a floodlight view. It creates broader, clearer, and more immediate visibility into how controls are functioning across the enterprise. This does not mean every leader sees every signal at once. It means the institution has the capacity to illuminate the control environment with enough precision and immediacy to govern intelligently.

The contrast can be framed clearly:

Dimension	**Legacy GRC (Snapshot)**	**Modern GRC (Continuous)**
Cadence	Periodic, annual or quarterly	Persistent, real time or event driven
Data Source	Manual samples and self-reporting	Direct telemetry and system logs
Response	Reactive remediation	Proactive prevention and automated control action
Visibility	Low resolution flashlight	High-definition floodlight

The significance of this shift cannot be overstated. Continuous control monitoring is not simply a better dashboard. It is the operating foundation of real time compliance. It changes oversight from an external review function into an embedded system capability. It allows governance to keep pace with automation. It allows trust to be preserved under velocity. And it gives the architect-leader something the snapshot model never truly could: a live line of sight into whether the institution is operating within its declared boundaries at the very moment those boundaries matter.

That is the beginning of real time compliance.

Event-Driven Oversight: The Governance Trigger

The technical heart of real-time compliance is not the dashboard, the report, or even the control library. It is the automated trigger. In a well-architected intelligent enterprise, every high-stakes action should have a corresponding governance event, a point at which the system must verify that required conditions have been met before execution is allowed to continue. This is where oversight ceases to be retrospective and becomes operational. Governance is no longer something applied after the action. It becomes a prerequisite for the action itself.

This is the essence of event-driven oversight.

In traditional compliance models, a transaction might be completed first and reviewed later. If a violation is discovered, remediation follows. In intelligent systems, that sequence is too slow. By the time the institution discovers that something should not have happened, the workflow may already have triggered downstream actions, created exposure, or introduced risk that is far more expensive to unwind. Event-driven oversight reverses the sequence. It asks not whether the organization can explain the action afterward, but whether the organization has designed the system so that the action cannot occur unless governance conditions are satisfied in real time.

Consider a practical example in automated vendor onboarding. An intelligent agent identifies a prospective vendor and prepares to advance the onboarding process. Under a legacy model, the onboarding action might proceed immediately, with compliance or security review occurring later through manual validation. Under a real-time compliance model, the impending action itself becomes the trigger. Before the onboarding API is ever called, a validation script retrieves the vendor's relevant security certificate or assurance artifact. The system then compares the certificate, configuration, or control evidence against enterprise standards, such as RSA encryption requirements, identity assurance thresholds, or other predefined control criteria. If the validation succeeds, the workflow continues within milliseconds. If it fails, the system freezes the process, records the event, and alerts the GRC portal or designated control owner for review.

What matters here is not simply the technical sequence. What matters is the architectural philosophy behind it. The compliance check is no longer an afterthought appended to workflow once the work is done. It is a gate built into the pathway of execution. The organization does not ask whether it can clean up noncompliant behavior later. It ensures the workflow cannot proceed in a noncompliant state at all. This is what safety by design means in practice.

That principle has implications far beyond vendor onboarding. The same logic can govern privileged access requests, automated financial approvals, data export actions, AI generated customer communications, identity federation events, model deployment workflows, and any other action in which speed without validation could create material institutional risk. Event-driven oversight allows the enterprise to transform policy from static documentation into active operational logic. Controls become dynamic. Oversight becomes immediate. Trust becomes enforceable at the moment of action rather than merely debatable afterward.

For the architect-leader, this is a decisive evolution in the meaning of governance. The most powerful oversight is no longer found in periodic review meetings or retrospective audit narratives. It is found in the design of the trigger itself, the point where action and accountability meet. When those triggers are well designed, governance ceases to be external friction and becomes part of the living intelligence of the enterprise.

Building the Kill Switch

As intelligent systems grow more autonomous, one leadership requirement becomes nonnegotiable: every meaningful system must have an out-of-bounds mechanism. In practical terms, this means the organization must possess the ability to halt, isolate, suspend, or revoke a system's authority the moment its behavior exceeds acceptable limits. That mechanism is the automated kill switch.

The phrase may sound dramatic, but the principle is straightforward. No responsible institution should grant persistent autonomy to a system without also defining the conditions under which autonomy can be withdrawn immediately. A kill switch is not evidence of mistrust in innovation. It is evidence of maturity in governance. It acknowledges a simple truth: the more speed, reach, and delegated agency a system possesses, the more important it becomes to preserve the enterprise's ability to intervene decisively when conditions begin to drift.

This is especially important because drift is rarely announced politely. An intelligent agent may begin showing signs of statistical bias. A model may start requesting unusually broad data access. A workflow may generate behavior outside its expected operating envelope. An orchestration layer may begin interacting with systems or datasets beyond its normal profile. A recommendation engine may suddenly produce outputs that remain technically plausible but strategically misaligned. In each case, waiting for quarterly review or manual investigation would be too slow. The governance layer must be capable of recognizing the deviation and acting immediately.

A mature kill switch is therefore more than an off button. It is a governed intervention mechanism. It may revoke a system's identity token, suspend API permissions, halt a workflow, isolate a service, redirect decisions to human review, disable access to sensitive data, or trigger containment protocols automatically. The point is not merely to stop the system. The point is to preserve institutional authority under conditions of uncertainty. The enterprise must remain capable of saying, in effect, no further action occurs until trust is restored.

This is one of the clearest examples of why governance should not be mischaracterized as anti-innovation. The automated kill switch does not exist to prevent the use of intelligent systems. It exists to make their use survivable at scale. Without a mechanism of rapid containment, organizations become hesitant to authorize autonomy because the consequences of error remain unbounded. With a kill switch, leaders can move more confidently because they know the architecture includes a means of stopping harm before it propagates into systemic failure.

There is also an important symbolic dimension to the kill switch. It embodies the principle that no system, however sophisticated, operates beyond the authority of the institution it serves. This matters because autonomous systems can easily create the illusion that control has been transferred permanently into the machinery itself. The kill switch rejects that illusion. It reminds the organization that intelligence remains subordinate to governance, and that delegated agency remains conditional rather than absolute.

For the architect-leader, the kill switch is one of the most powerful tools of responsible modern leadership. It reflects humility about the limits of prediction, discipline about the need for bounded autonomy, and seriousness about the enterprise's duty to protect itself from systemic rot. In an environment where intelligent systems are expected to move fast, adapt continuously, and operate across critical workflows, the kill switch is not a sign of fear. It is a sign that leadership understands how to preserve trust while still permitting velocity.

Conclusion: From Policing to Orchestrating

Real-time compliance changes more than the mechanics of oversight. It changes the role of the leader.

In the older model, leadership often functioned like policing after the fact. The organization acted, evidence accumulated, auditors reconstructed events, and leaders responded to reports that described what had already gone wrong. Compliance was retrospective by design. It depended on documentation, remediation, and the slow reconstruction of past conditions. In that world, the leader often encountered failure through the postmortem.

That model is now giving way to something far more dynamic. When compliance becomes real time, leadership can no longer remain tied to episodic inspection. The leader is no longer merely an auditor of institutional history. The leader becomes an orchestrator of living control systems and, in a very real sense, a pilot of enterprise motion. Instead of reading static reports about what happened last quarter, the leader now works from a flight dashboard, a live operating view of whether the institution is moving within safe, trusted, and governable parameters as events unfold.

This transition carries enormous implications. A pilot does not stare passively at instruments. A pilot interprets signals, distinguishes normal turbulence from structural danger, and responds with discipline rather than panic. The same must now be true of executive leadership in intelligent systems environments. Real-time compliance produces a constant stream of telemetry, validations, exceptions, alerts, and automated handshakes. The leader's task is not to react impulsively to every signal, but to understand what kind of signal is being observed and what level of response it requires.

That demands a new form of technical literacy. The architect-leader must be able to distinguish between a technical glitch and a governance breach. A temporary API timeout, a transient service interruption, or a recoverable system delay may require attention, but not necessarily escalation at the level of institutional control. A governance breach is different. It signals a systemic failure of logic, policy, thresholds, permissions, or oversight architecture. It suggests that the system is not merely malfunctioning but operating outside the boundaries of trust that justify its autonomy in the first place.

This distinction is essential to preserving the velocity of trust. If leaders trigger the kill switch for every minor glitch, the enterprise becomes paralyzed by overreaction. Systems lose autonomy, teams lose confidence, and the organization reverts to friction as a substitute for judgment. But if leaders fail to recognize or respond decisively to a true governance breach, the consequences are far more severe. Trust collapses, exposure spreads, and the legitimacy of both the system and its leadership may be damaged at once. Mature leadership requires the ability to know the difference and to act proportionately.

This is why real-time compliance is not simply a better control model. It is a leadership transformation. It shifts the executive posture from retrospective review to active navigation. It requires leaders to move beyond the old identity of inspector and into a new identity shaped by orchestration, interpretation, and disciplined intervention. Governance becomes less about hunting for past mistakes and more about maintaining live control over a self-correcting environment.

When compliance is automated and embedded into workflow, it ceases to function primarily as an administrative burden. It becomes a telemetry stream. It provides the clarity required for leaders to trust intelligent systems at scale, not because risk has disappeared, but because risk has become observable, governable, and interruptible in real time. The organization no longer relies on snapshots of yesterday. It gains a living view of whether its systems are acting within declared boundaries now.

That clarity, however, introduces the next great challenge. Real-time compliance can generate extraordinary volumes of data, but data alone does not create understanding. Where does all of that telemetry go. How is it organized, prioritized, and rendered intelligible to human leadership. How does the enterprise transform millions of automated control events into a usable operating picture rather than a flood of noise.

Those questions lead directly into the next chapter. Real-time compliance creates the signals of trust. The next task is building the visibility architecture through which those signals can be seen, interpreted, and governed.

5: The Workflow Portal

The Fog of Automation

By 2026, the average enterprise is no longer a neatly bounded organization supported by a small number of visible systems. It is a dense, shifting web of cloud functions, orchestration layers, third party agents, SaaS dependencies, legacy databases, embedded scripts, identity services, compliance engines, and API driven interactions moving across multiple environments at once. Azure functions trigger downstream actions in one part of the architecture. AWS Lambda scripts execute event based logic in another. Third party AI agents perform classification, summarization, or workflow routing. Legacy SQL databases continue to supply institutional memory from an earlier era. Each component may function reasonably well on its own, yet from the vantage point of leadership the whole can begin to resemble less an integrated enterprise and more a dispersed field of invisible motion.

This is the new condition of organizational complexity. The challenge is no longer merely that systems are advanced. The challenge is that they are fragmented, distributed, and often operationally opaque to the very people charged with governing them. A single business outcome may now depend on dozens of system interactions taking place across multiple providers, control planes, and logic layers. The path from decision to action is rarely linear. It is mediated by handoffs, validations, policies, tokens, scripts, and automated calls that few leaders can observe directly in ordinary workflow. As a result, the modern executive often presides over an enterprise that is functioning continuously yet remains only partially visible.

That invisibility creates what may be called the fog of automation.

Fog is not simply the presence of complexity. Fog is complexity without line of sight. It is the condition in which motion is occurring, decisions are being made, risks are accumulating, and systems are interacting, yet no single human perspective can easily trace what is happening with sufficient clarity to govern it well. In such environments, oversight begins to degrade not because leadership is weak, but because the architecture has outgrown the institution's ability to see it coherently. Fragmentation becomes the enemy of judgment. Distributed execution becomes the enemy of accountability. And the more the enterprise relies on automation without unified visibility, the more leadership risks become symbolic rather than operational.

This is why visibility is no longer a secondary convenience. It is a condition of executive authority. A leader cannot govern what cannot be seen in a timely, intelligible, and actionable form. When workflows are scattered across environments, logs are stored in separate tools, control signals appear in isolated dashboards, and exceptions surface through disconnected channels, leadership is forced into a reactive posture. Time is lost not only in system delay, but in interpretive delay. The institution does not merely suffer from technical fragmentation. It suffers from decision fragmentation.

The answer to this problem is not simply more dashboards. It is the creation of a unifying operational surface through which the enterprise becomes governable again. That surface is the workflow portal.

The workflow portal is the centralized command center of the intelligent enterprise. It is the place where technical telemetry is translated into strategic decision making. It gathers the signals of automation, governance, and intervention into a coherent operating view that leadership can actually use. Properly understood, it is not merely a reporting interface or an attractive dashboard layered on top of system activity. It is a truth engine. Its purpose is to provide sufficient line of sight into the automated heart of the company so that speed does not outrun understanding and complexity does not dissolve accountability.

This distinction matters. A dashboard may display metrics. A workflow portal must support governance. A dashboard may inform. A portal must orient. A dashboard may summarize yesterday. A portal must help leadership understand what is happening now, what requires attention, what is drifting out of bounds, and what strategic decisions are emerging from the underlying machinery of the enterprise. In that sense, the workflow portal is one of the most important visibility structures in the entire architecture of intelligent leadership.

The architect-leader does not need to see every technical event in raw form. But the leader does need a governing surface that makes the enterprise legible at the level where decisions can be made with confidence. Without such a surface, the organization remains trapped in the fog of automation. With it, the enterprise begins to recover one of the most precious assets in the age of intelligent systems: clarity.

The Single Pane of Glass

The aim of a high-performance workflow portal is often described through a familiar phrase: a single pane of glass. The phrase is useful, but it is often misunderstood. It does not simply mean placing more metrics on one screen. It means creating a unified operational view through which the leader can understand the state of the intelligent enterprise without losing time, judgment, or situational awareness to fragmentation.

In a traditional technology environment, executives and managers could often tolerate a degree of observational separation. Security logs might live in one application, compliance reports in another, operational metrics in a third, and business outcomes in yet another reporting layer. Because workflows moved more slowly, leaders could afford a certain amount of context switching. They could assemble an understanding by moving from one system to another, reconciling information manually, and forming a decision over time. In a high velocity environment, that model breaks down.

Context switching is no longer a minor inconvenience. It becomes a form of leadership latency.

When an executive must move across multiple interfaces to determine what the system is doing, whether it is doing it within policy, and whether intervention is required, precious time is lost. More importantly, coherence is lost. Signals that should be interpreted together are instead encountered separately. Operational activity is viewed without governance context. Compliance status is reviewed without workflow context. Human escalation needs are discovered only after the system has already moved past the point where early intervention would have mattered most. In such conditions, the organization may possess abundant information and remain strategically disoriented.

The single pane of glass is meant to correct this. It provides a unified decision surface in which the most important dimensions of enterprise activity are visible together rather than in isolation. For the architect-leader, at least three streams of information must be brought into one view.

The first is *operational telemetry*. This answers the question, what is the system doing right now? Leaders must be able to see the active state of the enterprise in motion. How many workflows are running. Which agents are active. What volumes are being processed. Where are delays emerging. What dependencies are being called. What load is the system carrying. Operational telemetry gives leadership visibility into live activity rather than retrospective abstraction. It reveals whether the system is functioning, scaling, or straining under present conditions.

The second is *compliance status*. This answers the question, is the system doing its work correctly and within approved boundaries? Operational speed alone is never sufficient. Leaders must know whether the workflows currently in motion are meeting control requirements, honoring policy thresholds, maintaining encryption standards, preserving access restrictions, and behaving within the institution's acceptable risk posture. A portal that shows activity without compliance is merely a performance surface. A true workflow portal shows activity and governance together, allowing leaders to see not only that the machine is moving, but that it is moving lawfully, safely, and in alignment with institutional expectations.

The third is *human intervention points*. This answers the question, where does the system need me or my team? Not every event deserves executive attention. Not every exception requires immediate escalation. But the portal must clearly surface the moments where machine speed reaches the boundary of delegated authority and human judgment must reenter the process. This may include a high-risk vendor assessment, an anomalous data access request, a confidence score falling below a threshold, a policy conflict requiring exception approval, or an automation path that has triggered a governance handoff. These intervention points are critical because they transform the portal from a passive display into an active instrument of leadership.

Taken together, these three streams form the core of the single pane of glass. The portal must reveal what the system is doing, whether it is doing it correctly, and where leadership must act. If even one of these dimensions is missing, the view becomes incomplete. Operational telemetry without compliance status produces speed without trust. Compliance status without operational telemetry produces governance without context. Without intervention clarity produce visibility without actionability. The power of the portal lies in integration.

This is why the workflow portal should be understood as more than an efficiency tool. It is an antidote to fragmentation. It reduces leadership latency by collapsing multiple interpretive burdens into one coherent decision environment. It allows the architect-leader to move from scattered observation to disciplined situational awareness. And in an enterprise where millions of automated handshakes may occur every day, that coherence is not cosmetic. It is foundational to maintain the velocity of trust.

The single pane of glass, at its best, does not merely simplify reporting. It restores governability to a distributed enterprise.

Data Orchestration: From Noise to Insight

A workflow portal that merely displays raw data is not an instrument of leadership. It is a liability disguised as visibility. Most modern enterprises do not suffer from a shortage of information. They suffer from an excess of fragmented, unprioritized, and context poor information. Leaders are already surrounded by dashboards, reports, alerts, logs, metrics, and status feeds. The problem is rarely access to data. The problem is the absence of clarity.

This is why the workflow portal must function as more than a viewing surface. It must operate as a *data orchestrator*. Its role is not simply to expose activity, but to transform overwhelming volumes of technical signal into a decision environment that a human leader can govern. In an intelligent enterprise, millions of automated transactions, validations, API calls, control checks, and workflow events may occur each day. If all that activity is surfaced in raw form, leadership is not empowered. It is buried.

The portal therefore performs one of the most important interpretive functions in the modern enterprise: it separates noise from signal. It filters routine activity, compresses repetitive events, and elevates only those conditions that carry governance significance, operational consequence, or strategic relevance. In that sense, the portal is not simply reporting the state of the system. It is curating the state of the system in a way that preserves executive attention for the moments that matter most.

A powerful way to achieve this is through *threshold based reporting*. Rather than forcing leaders to process every event at the same level of urgency, the portal organizes system behavior into graduated states of significance.

At the **green** level, the system is operating within defined governance, risk, and compliance parameters. Workflows are proceeding as expected. Controls are passing. Telemetry is stable. No leadership action is required. Green is not silence. It is governed normalcy. It reassures the leader that the architecture is performing as designed.

At the **yellow** level, the system is approaching a threshold that may require awareness but not yet intervention. This might include a rise in data usage, a mild drift in compliance behavior, an unusual but not yet critical change in workflow latency, or an increase in exception volume that remains within tolerable bounds. Yellow exists to preserve foresight. It tells the leader that the system is beginning to move toward a condition that deserves observation. The objective is not to create alarm, but to create awareness early enough that corrective action can occur before disruption becomes necessary.

At the **red** level, the system has crossed into a condition that requires decisive response. A kill switch event may have been triggered. A significant logic failure may have occurred. A control threshold may have been violated. A workflow may have entered an unauthorized state. Red is the point at which the portal stops functioning merely as an observation surface and becomes a demand for leadership action. It signals that the boundaries of trusted autonomy have been exceeded and that institutional authority must reenter the process immediately.

This graduated model is essential because it allows leaders to govern by exception rather than by exhaustion. That distinction cannot be overstated. In low maturity environments, leaders are often forced into a posture of constant review because the system has not been designed to tell them what matters most. The result is cognitive overload, decision fatigue, and a gradual erosion of confidence in the visibility environment itself. When everything is urgent, nothing is meaningfully actionable.

By contrast, a well-orchestrated portal preserves executive focus. It makes normal operations visible without demanding constant attention. It surfaces emerging issues before they become crises. It elevates genuine risks with unmistakable clarity. In doing so, it converts visibility into governability. The leader is no longer drowning in data. The leader is navigating through structured significance.

This is one of the most underappreciated dimensions of intelligent enterprise design. True visibility is not the raw exposure of everything. True visibility is the disciplined presentation of what matters, when it matters, at the level of action it requires. That is the shift from noise to insight. And that is the work of orchestration.

The Quantified Alert Framework

A workflow portal succeeds or fails not by how much data it can display, but by how effectively it converts visibility into action. In the intelligent enterprise, the central challenge is not the absence of information. It is the burden of determining which signals deserve human attention and which do not. A portal that presents everything with equal urgency quickly becomes unusable. A portal that hides meaningful anomalies beneath routine activity becomes dangerous. What leadership requires is a disciplined framework for actionability.

That actionability can be understood through the density of visibility. Put simply, the value of a portal view rises when meaningful signals are elevated clearly and noise is reduced aggressively. The architect-leader's objective is therefore twofold. The denominator, noise, must be minimized so that the portal does not drown its users in routine or low value information. At the same time, the numerator, meaningful signals, must never fall to zero when a genuine risk is present. If important anomalies disappear inside summarization, compression, or filtering logic, then the portal may appear elegant while quietly failing its governing purpose.

This tension defines the quantified alert framework. The goal is not maximal alerting. It is calibrated alerting. A mature portal should surface conditions only when the trust threshold has been approached, strained, or breached. That means the system demands human cognitive load only when human judgment is genuinely required. Routine behavior remains visible in aggregate, but not disruptive. Emerging drift is surfaced early enough to preserve foresight. Material failures are elevated unmistakably. In this way, the portal supports management by exception rather than management by interruption.

This distinction matters because cognitive bandwidth is now one of the scarcest resources in executive leadership. In fragmented environments, leaders are too often forced to spend attention on noise because the system has not been disciplined enough to present significance hierarchically. The result is either fatigue or desensitization. Alert fatigue causes leaders to miss what matters because too much urgently appears. Desensitization causes them to underreact because repeated noise trains them to distrust the visibility environment itself. Neither condition is compatible with trustworthy speed.

A well-designed quantified alert framework prevents both failures. It gives structure to attention. It ensures that when the portal speaks with urgency, leadership can trust that something meaningful has happened. It also ensures that the absence of an alert is not a blind spot, but evidence that the workflow remains within governed parameters. In that sense, the portal becomes more than a screen. It becomes a disciplined filter between the overwhelming volume of machine activity and the finite interpretive capacity of human leadership.

This is one of the deepest principles of the workflow portal. Visibility alone is not enough. Visibility must be scored, prioritized, and made proportionate to institutional consequence. Only then can the portal become truly actionable.

The Psychology of Systemic Transparency

The move from black box automation to portal led oversight changes not only how the enterprise is governed, but how it thinks. Visibility alters behavior. When actions, validations, thresholds, and exceptions remain hidden inside scattered systems, teams naturally optimize for speed, local efficiency, and task completion. In low visibility environments, it is easy for minor compliance drift to be dismissed as negligible, for procedural shortcuts to seem harmless, and for technical teams to assume that small deviations will remain buried inside complexity.

That psychology begins to change the moment the enterprise adopts systemic transparency.

When every automated handshake, policy check, exception route, and governance gate is visualized in real time through a shared operational surface, organizational behavior becomes more disciplined. Decisions are no longer isolated within private technical domains. They become part of a visible institutional record. That visibility encourages a shift away from unchecked velocity and toward systemic quality. Teams become more careful not simply because they are being watched, but because the operating environment now makes consequences and deviations legible in a shared way.

This is where the workflow portal begins to function as more than an operational tool. It becomes a cultural anchor. It gives tangible expression to the enterprise's risk appetite, quality standards, and ethical commitments. It shows, in daily operational form, what the organization actually means when it claims to value trust, integrity, and responsible automation. Those values are no longer left floating at the level of policy language or executive aspiration. They are made visible at the point of execution.

For the architect-leader, this is one of the most consequential effects of systemic transparency. Culture can no longer be treated as something separate from the machinery of the enterprise. In intelligent systems environments, culture is reflected in thresholds, escalation paths, exception handling, logging fidelity, and the visible treatment of risk. The portal keeps those institutional commitments in view even as millions of autonomous actions take place beneath the surface of the company. It reminds the enterprise that scale does not excuse opacity and that speed does not remove the obligation to remain accountable.

A transparent system therefore creates more serious organization. It encourages better design, more responsible routing, clearer exception handling, and greater respect for policy because the enterprise can see itself operating. That visibility does not eliminate failure, but it raises the standard for how failure is understood, addressed, and prevented. In that sense, systemic transparency is not merely informative. It is formative. It shapes the habits of the enterprise over time.

The Immutable Audit: Your Digital Legal Counsel

By 2026, regulatory scrutiny is no longer satisfied by periodic check-ins, static policy binders, or retrospective narrative explanations. Oversight has entered the era of algorithmic discovery. When an intelligent system fails, the first question from regulators, auditors, investigators, or opposing counsel is rarely whether the organization had a written policy. The first real question is whether the organization can reconstruct what actually happened with sufficient precision to demonstrate control, trace responsibility, and establish the integrity of its operating logic.

In that environment, log fidelity becomes one of the most important forms of institutional self-protection.

This is why the workflow portal must function as an immutable audit layer. It serves not merely as an operational visibility tool, but as the searchable, durable record of systemic decision making. Properly designed, it captures the DNA of every meaningful automated action and preserves the evidence required to explain, defend, and, if necessary, challenge what the system did.

That record begins with *provenance*. Which data source triggered the action. What event, dataset, request, or workflow input initiated the process. Without provenance, the organization cannot establish whether the system acted on trusted information or contaminated input.

It continues with *inference*. What logic, model behavior, rule set, or decision path shaped the output. The organization may not always be able to expose every microscopic parameter of a complex model, but it must still be able to explain the operational logic that guided the action in a way that is defensible and intelligible.

It also captures *governance*. Which control gate, threshold, policy validation, or compliance checkpoint approved the move. This matters because regulators and auditors increasingly care less about the existence of a library control in theory and more about whether controls were actually active at the point of execution.

Finally, it preserves *authorization*. Who, whether human or machine identity, signed off on the execution. In intelligent systems environments, identity and authority can no longer be assumed. They must be attributable. The enterprise must know not only that an action occurred, but under whose delegated authority it proceeded.

When these elements are centralized inside a searchable, executive friendly interface, compliance undergoes a profound transformation. It stops functioning merely as a defensive cost center that produces documentation on demand. It becomes a strategic, auditable asset. The institution gains the ability to defend itself with evidence rather than narrative alone. It can reconstruct events quickly, distinguish glitches from breach, support legal response, satisfy regulatory inquiry, and strengthen internal learning after incidents occur.

This is why the immutable audit is so important to the architect-leader. In an intelligent enterprise, legal defensibility and operational clarity increasingly depend on the same thing: a trustworthy record of how the system behaved. The workflow portal, when built well, becomes something like digital legal counsel embedded into the operating environment itself. It preserves not just activity, but accountability.

Conclusion: Reclaiming the Helm

The workflow portal is the physical manifestation of leadership architecture in the intelligent enterprise. It is the means by which the chaos of distributed agency, fragmented telemetry, and machine speed is brought back into a form that can be governed. Without it, the executive risks becoming a passenger inside a company increasingly shaped by invisible processes and automated decisions. With it, leadership begins to reclaim the helm.

That is the deeper significance of the portal. It centralizes the complexity of the enterprise into a truth engine, a place where activity, governance, intervention, and accountability can be seen together. It gives the architect-leader something more valuable than data alone. It gives orientation. It allows the enterprise to move from scattered observation to disciplined situational awareness, from reaction to orchestration, and from symbolic oversight to active control.

Yet visibility, while indispensable, is only half the battle. Seeing the system's decisions does not by itself resolve the most difficult question of the intelligent age. Once an action has been traced, once the logic has been surfaced, and once the workflow can be seen clearly, another challenge immediately emerges. Who is responsible when the machine makes a mistake. Who bears accountability when delegated agency produces harm, drift, or unintended consequence. And how should leadership think about legal and ethical responsibility in a world where action is increasingly shared between human design and machine execution.

Those questions lead directly into the next chapter. In Chapter 6, the discussion moves from interface to intellect, from visibility to responsibility, and into one of the defining legal and ethical challenges of intelligent systems: algorithmic accountability.

6: Algorithmic Accountability

The "Algorithm Made Me Do It" Defense Is Dead

In the early period of automated decision making, organizations benefited from a convenient form of legal and ethical fog. When a system denied a loan, flagged a security clearance, misclassified a risk, or generated a flawed supply chain recommendation, leaders often pointed to complexity itself as though it were an explanation. The model was described as too advanced, too multidimensional, or too opaque for ordinary human interpretation. The black box became more than a technical metaphor. It became a cultural defense mechanism. Complexity was invoked not merely to describe the system, but to dilute responsibility for its consequences.

That era is ending.

By 2026, the environment surrounding intelligent systems has changed dramatically. Regulators, oversight bodies, auditors, boards, and institutional stakeholders have grown far less willing to accept opacity as an excuse for avoidable harm. Whether the setting is commercial, governmental, defense related, financial, or operational, a clearer principle is now taking hold: accountability cannot be delegated simply because execution has been automated. Institutions may assign tasks to intelligent systems, but they do not thereby surrender ownership of the outcomes those systems produce. Delegated execution does not erase human responsibility. It intensifies the obligation to govern the conditions under which execution occurs.

This is the defining legal and ethical shift of the intelligent systems era. The question is no longer whether an algorithm was involved. The question is who authorized its use, who defined its boundaries, who approved its integration into workflow, who accepted its risk profile, and who remained responsible for the results once it began to act in the name of the enterprise. In other words, the presence of automation no longer obscures leadership responsibility. It sharpens it.

This matters because intelligent systems now sit much closer to consequential action than earlier generations of automation ever did. They recommend, classify, prioritize, deny, escalate, allocate, and in some cases trigger downstream actions with little human delay. When those actions affect money, access, compliance status, security posture, procurement outcomes, customer treatment, workforce decisions, or public trust, the cost of ambiguity grows rapidly. A poorly governed system can produce a multimillion-dollar compliance error, expose sensitive information, embed bias into critical processes, or create downstream harm that only becomes visible long after the automated decision has already propagated. In such circumstances, the black box is no longer a shield. It is evidence that leadership failed to build the level of visibility, traceability, and control that the environment now demands.

This is why the phrase "the algorithm made me do it" has become intellectually and institutionally indefensible. Algorithms do not appoint themselves. Models do not define their own risk appetite. Workflows do not grant themselves authority. Those are design choices. Governance choices. Leadership choices. When institutions rely on systems whose outputs they cannot explain at a level sufficient for accountability, they are not absolved by that complexity. They are exposed by it.

The architect-leader must therefore adopt a new posture toward automated decision making. The task is no longer merely to ask whether the system is technically capable. It is to ask whether the system is governable, defensible, and attributable. Can the organization explain how the system was authorized, what data it used, what logic shaped its action, what controls constrained it, and who remained responsible when the outcome reached the real world. If the answer is no, then the issue is not simply technological opacity. It is institutional negligence masquerading as sophistication.

This is the deeper meaning of algorithmic accountability. It is the insistence that power delegated into machines does not cease to be human power. It remains organizational power, exercised through technical means and therefore answerable to the same standards of stewardship, legality, and ethical seriousness that apply to any other consequential act of leadership.

The Liability Gap: Speed Versus Responsibility

The central challenge of algorithmic accountability is not only that intelligent systems are powerful. It is that they operate on a radically different timescale from the legal, ethical, and investigative processes meant to govern them. An intelligent system may classify, infer, approve, deny, escalate, or trigger action in milliseconds. The organizational harm resulting from that action may not become visible for weeks or months. The legal inquiry into what occurred may then unfold over years. Between machine speed and human accountability lies a dangerous interval of exposure.

This is the liability gap.

The liability gap emerges because action and understanding are no longer synchronized. The system acts immediately, but the institution often understands only belatedly. Harm accumulates while the organization is still reconstructing the chain of events. Customers may already be affected. Compliance obligations may already be breached. Security weaknesses may already have been exploited. Reputational damage may already be circulating. By the time human investigators begin asking what happened, the workflow has long since moved on, and the enterprise is left trying to reverse engineer decisions that were made at speeds no ordinary manual review process was built to match.

This temporal mismatch is one of the most destabilizing features of the intelligent enterprise. In older operating models, many important decisions unfolded slowly enough that intervention, review, or second thought could still occur before consequences widened. In intelligent systems, the sequence is compressed. Inference becomes action. Action becomes consequence. Consequence becomes exposure. Each stage may unfold before human governance has meaningfully entered the loop. The result is an accountability problem that is not merely legal, but architectural. Institutions are expected to answer for outcomes they may not yet be able to explain in real time.

Bridging this gap requires something more rigorous than policy language or post incident narrative. It requires *forensic governance.*

Forensic governance is the discipline of designing intelligent systems so that every meaningful inference, recommendation, or action leaves behind a trace that can later be reconstructed, examined, and defended. It is not enough to know that a system acted. The organization must be able to know why it acted, what conditions shaped that action, what controls were present at the moment of execution, and whether the resulting outcome remained within the enterprise's accepted boundaries of authority and risk. Forensic governance makes accountability possible by preserving the evidence required to connect machine speed with human responsibility.

At the center of this discipline is the idea of a *reasoning trace.* Every consequential algorithmic action should be accompanied by a structured record of its decision path. That record may include the relevant inputs, the governing data sources, the logic or model pathway applied, the threshold or confidence conditions met, the policy controls triggered, the workflow route taken, and the human or machine identity under whose authority the action proceeded. The purpose is not to pretend that every advanced system can be reduced to perfect intuitive simplicity. The purpose is to ensure that the organization can reconstruct enough of the decision anatomy to establish accountability after the fact and, ideally, to improve governance before the next failure occurs.

This marks an important evolution in leadership itself. Too many institutions still operate with what might be called stochastic leadership, a style of governance in which leaders accept probabilistic outcomes without building sufficient mechanisms for verification, traceability, and intervention. They know the system is likely to perform well most of the time, and they trust that aggregate performance is enough. But aggregate performance is not a defense when a specific decision causes material harm. What is now required is a more deterministic form of oversight, one grounded not in blind confidence that the model usually works, but in verifiable evidence of how the system behaved in each consequential case.

Deterministic oversight does not mean eliminating every probabilistic element from intelligent systems. That would be unrealistic. It means ensuring that when probabilistic systems are used, the governance environment around them remains structured enough to support attribution, explanation, and legal defensibility. In effect, the enterprise must build determinism around stochastic components. The model may remain probabilistic, but the oversight architecture cannot be.

For the architect-leader, this is a defining responsibility. The challenge is not merely to accelerate decision making. It is to ensure that speed does not sever responsibility from action. The organization must be able to bridge the time gap between what the machine did instantly and what the institution may spend months or years answering for later. That bridge is built through forensic governance, reasoning traceability, and the discipline of designing systems whose decisions can be accounted for long after the moment of execution has passed.

That is where algorithmic accountability truly begins.

Explainable AI as a Leadership Requirement

For many years, explainable AI was treated as a specialized concern, something reserved for data scientists, model researchers, or technical teams working close to algorithm design. It was often framed as an academic or methodological issue rather than an executive one. In the age of intelligent systems, that distinction no longer holds. Explainability has moved from the margins of technical inquiry to the center of leadership responsibility.

The reason is straightforward. An enterprise cannot claim to govern what it cannot meaningfully explain. If a leader cannot account for why a system produced a decision, recommendation, classification, or escalation, then the institution's control over that system is already weaker than it appears. Performance alone is no longer enough. Accuracy alone is no longer enough. Even efficiency alone is no longer enough. In environments where intelligent systems influence consequential outcomes, leadership must be able to answer the question beneath the output: why did the system do what it did.

This is where explainable AI becomes indispensable. Explainability does not mean reducing every advanced model into a simplistic mechanical narrative. Nor does it require every executive to master the internal mathematics of neural architecture. What it does require is the creation of a governance environment in which the logic surrounding a decision can be made visible enough to support oversight, challenge, remediation, and accountability. Explainability, in that sense, is the glass cage around the black box. It does not deny that complexity exists. It ensures that complexity does not become an excuse for surrendered authority.

From a leadership perspective, explainable AI matters because it restores interpretive control. It gives executives and oversight teams a way to move from mere observation of outcomes to structured understanding of causes. When used properly, it allows leadership to ask not only what the system concluded, but what factors most influenced that conclusion, what alternative conditions might have changed it, and why a specific case moved the way it did. That shift is essential because without it, the organization remains dependent on outputs it may be unable to defend under scrutiny.

Several forms of explainability are especially important for executive oversight.

The first is *feature attribution*. This identifies which data elements most heavily influenced a system's decision. In a vendor assessment, for example, leadership may need to know whether the model's country of origin weighted more heavily than encryption standards, or whether network exposure, contractual history, or control maturity drove the classification. Feature attribution matters because it reveals what the system is prioritizing in practice, which may or may not match what the organization intended it to prioritize in policy.

The second is *counterfactual analysis*. This addresses one of the most useful accountability questions in intelligent systems: what would have needed to change for the system to reach a different conclusion. Counterfactual reasoning is powerful because it does not merely describe the decision after the fact. It reveals the structure of the decision boundary itself. It helps leaders understand whether the outcome turned on a minor threshold issue, a material risk factor, or a combination of conditions that made the decision effectively inevitable. In practical governance terms, counterfactuals help distinguish between stable system logic and fragile or overly sensitive model behavior.

The third is *local interpretability*. This focuses not on the behavior of the model in the abstract, but on why the system made this specific decision in this specific case. Local interpretability is often where accountability becomes most actionable because institutions are rarely judged only on model performance in aggregate. They are judged on what happened in particular consequential moments. A regulator, auditor, board member, or affected stakeholder does not ask only whether the model usually performs well. They ask why this applicant was denied, why this vendor was flagged, why this alert was ignored, or why this workflow executed when it did. Local interpretability is the level at which technical explanation meets legal and ethical relevance.

Together, these capabilities form a spectrum from opacity to transparency, from black box uncertainty to clear box accountability. The exact level of explainability required will vary by context, but the principle does not. The more consequential the system's role, the greater the leadership obligation to ensure that its decisions can be interpreted at a level sufficient for governance.

For the architect-leader, explainability is therefore not a specialized analytics feature. It is a condition of responsible authority. It is what allows the enterprise to preserve confidence in systems without lapsing into blind trust. It is what enables challenge without requiring paralysis. Most importantly, it is what allows leadership to retain the ability to say, with credibility, that the organization remains in control of the systems acting in its name.

The Accountability Matrix

One of the most dangerous mistakes organizations make with intelligent systems is to treat accountability as though it were a binary question. Either the human is responsible or the machine is responsible. Either the human is in the loop or the human is out of the loop. Either the system is autonomous or it is not. In practice, none of these simplifications are sufficient. Accountability in intelligent systems is not binary. It is architectural. It varies according to the level of autonomy granted, the timing of human intervention, the design of the workflow, and the degree to which the enterprise has embedded governance into the path of execution.

This is why the architect-leader must define accountability explicitly rather than assume it implicitly. The location of the human in the loop must be named, structured, and governed in advance. If it is not, then responsibility will become diffuse precisely when the institution can least afford ambiguity. The purpose of an accountability matrix is to prevent that diffusion by clarifying who owns the outcome at each level of system autonomy.

At the first level is *human directed* operation. Here, the system suggests, ranks, summarizes, or recommends, but the human makes the actual decision. The machine provides support. The human remains the clear point of judgment and execution. In this model, accountability rests primarily with the human operator because the intelligent system has not been granted decisive authority. The system informs. The person decides. This is often the most appropriate structure for high consequence decisions in environments where human interpretation remains indispensable.

At the second level is *human delegated* operation. In this model, the system makes the decision, but the human is given a short window to intervene or veto before execution becomes final. This is a meaningful shift because authorities have now moved closer to the machine, even though human override remains available. Here, accountability often begins to migrate from the frontline operator to the system architect or design owner, because the critical question is no longer simply whether the human reacted in time. It is whether the workflow, thresholds, and veto structure were designed responsibly in the first place. When humans are given only a narrow intervention window, architecture becomes destiny.

At the third level is *human governed* operation. The system decides and acts, while the human reviews logs, trends, or exception reports on a periodic basis. Human presence remains in governance, but not in immediate decision execution. This model can be appropriate for bounded, repetitive, lower ambiguity processes where the institution has developed strong confidence in system consistency and control maturity. At this level, accountability often sits with a governance executive such as the Chief Risk Officer or equivalent control authority, because the organization has formally accepted a structure in which oversight is retrospective and systemic rather than immediate and transactional.

At the fourth level is **full autonomy** within strict boundaries. Here, the system decides and acts without routine human review at the point of execution, operating only within predefined kill switch parameters, thresholds, and governance constraints. This is the most demanding accountability posture because the organization has effectively authorized the machine to carry delegated agency at scale. In such environments, accountability cannot be diffused downward. It ultimately resides at the highest level of institutional authority, often the board or top executive governance body, because the decision to permit that degree of autonomy is itself a strategic and fiduciary act.

The logic of the matrix can be summarized clearly:

Level of Autonomy	**Definition**	**Accountability Owner**
Human Directed	The system suggests, the human decides	The human operator
Human Delegated	The system decides, the human may veto within a short window	The system architect
Human Governed	The system decides and acts, the human reviews periodically	The Chief Risk Officer

Level of Autonomy	Definition	Accountability Owner
Full Autonomy	The system decides and acts within strict kill switch boundaries	The Board of Directors

What makes this framework so important is that it reveals a critical principle: as autonomy increases, the technical requirement for governance guardrails rises exponentially. Higher autonomy demands higher fidelity accountability. It is not enough to say that a more advanced system is more capable. The institution must also prove that the corresponding escalation logic, auditability, explainability, kill switches, reasoning traces, and authorization structures are mature enough to justify the autonomy being granted.

This is where many organizations fail. They increase system autonomy without proportionately increasing governance precision. They permit machines to act faster and more independently while leaving accountability models vague, inherited, or underdeveloped. The result is a dangerous mismatch between operational power and institutional control. When failure occurs, everyone asks who was responsible, only to discover that no one had clearly defined the answer in advance.

The architect-leader does not allow that ambiguity to persist. Accountability must be designed with the same rigor as workflow, telemetry, and control logic. The question is never simply whether a human remains somewhere in the loop. The question is where, when, with what authority, under what time constraints, and with what evidentiary record. Only then can the enterprise say it has not merely deployed autonomy but governed it.

Coding Ethics into the Logic Gates

Organizations often speak about ethics in broad and aspirational terms. They frame it as a matter of culture, values, mission, or principle. Those dimensions matter, but in an intelligent enterprise they are no longer sufficient on their own. When systems are making or shaping consequential decisions at machine speed, ethics cannot remain only a philosophical commitment. It must be translated into functional parameters.

This is one of the defining responsibilities of the architect-leader. A value that cannot survive translation into workflow, policy logic, access controls, validation rules, and system constraints is not yet governing the enterprise. It may inspire the annual report. It may appear in the mission statement. It may guide executive rhetoric. But until it is embedded into the architecture of action, it remains vulnerable to being overridden by convenience, speed, or local optimization.

Consider a company that declares privacy first commitment. In a traditional environment, that promise might live primarily in policy manuals, training sessions, or customer messaging. In an intelligent system, that is not enough. Privacy must be made operational. It must appear in the code that controls access, in the configuration that governs data routing, in the script that masks personally identifiable information before it reaches the inference layer, in the policy engine that denies unauthorized requests, and in the workflow logic that prevents sensitive data from being exposed downstream. In other words, privacy must become something the system is structurally prevented from violating under ordinary conditions.

The same is true for fairness, transparency, proportionality, human dignity, security, and mission alignment. If an organization claims fairness as a core value, then fairness cannot remain a slogan. It must shape threshold design, model review, escalation logic, and bias testing procedures. If an organization claims transparency as a value, then reasoning traces, logging fidelity, and explainability requirements must be built into its oversight architecture. If it claims security as foundational, then identity, authorization, encryption, segmentation, and validation must be enforced not merely in policy language, but in the technical fabric of the workflow itself.

This is where ethics becomes operational discipline. Functional parameters are the point at which moral aspiration becomes executable governance. They convert values from abstract declarations into enforceable conditions of system behavior. They ensure that the machine does not merely act efficiently but acts within the boundaries of what the institution is willing to defend ethically, legally, and strategically.

For the architect-leader, this is one of the clearest tests of real authority. It is not enough to approve ethical principles at the policy level and assume someone else will figure out how to reflect them in the operating environment. Leadership must ensure that corporate values are translated into the logic gates of infrastructure. Values must become thresholds. Principles must become validations. Risk appetite must become constraints. Ethical commitments must become workflow conditions. Only then can the institution say with credibility that its systems are acting in alignment with its declared intent.

This is the deeper meaning of accountable design. The leader proves seriousness not by speaking eloquently about ethics, but by ensuring that system execution is incapable, under normal operation, of drifting casually away from the enterprise's governing values. The system's intent must be hard coded into its execution. That is where leadership ceases to be rhetorical and becomes architectural.

The Vanity of Unchecked Efficiency

One of the great temptations of the intelligent enterprise is to mistake efficiency for legitimacy. Automation promises lower cost, higher throughput, reduced friction, and extraordinary speed. Those gains are real, and in many cases they are necessary. Yet efficiency, left unexamined, can become one of the most deceptive metrics in modern leadership. A system may perform with remarkable precision, process enormous volumes of work, and eliminate large amounts of human effort while still moving the institution away from its deepest obligations.

This is where the warning behind the vanity of toil becomes so important. Motion is not meaning. Optimization is not wisdom. Scale is not moral seriousness. An enterprise that achieves perfect procedural efficiency while gradually eroding its ethical center is not demonstrating progress. It is building on sand. The danger is not merely that the organization will move too quickly. The danger is that it will become so impressed by its own technical capability that it stops asking whether the system still serves the mission it was built to advance.

Unchecked efficiency creates that distortion because metrics often reward what is measurable before they reward what is worthy. Throughput can be counted easily. Cost reduction can be quantified quickly. Cycle time can be benchmarked. But human dignity, fairness, trustworthiness, proportionality, and ethical coherence require a different kind of judgment. They are harder to compress into simple dashboards, and therefore easier for institutions to neglect when speed becomes the dominant value.

Algorithmic accountability functions as an anchor of reality against that drift. It forces the enterprise to ask harder questions than whether the system works. It asks whether the system deserves to work at scale. It asks whether automation is serving the mission or merely serving the metrics. It asks whether the organization is becoming more effective in any meaningful sense, or simply more efficient at producing outcomes it may not ultimately be willing to defend.

That is why accountability is not the enemy of performance. It is the discipline that keeps performance connected to purpose. It ensures that the intelligent system remains a tool in service of human flourishing rather than an engine of systemic harm. It prevents leadership from surrendering moral responsibility to the seduction of speed. And it reminds the enterprise that a system should not be judged only by what it can do, but by what it is authorized, structured, and worthy to do.

For the architect-leader, this is the final test of seriousness in the age of intelligent systems. The task is not merely to build fast systems, accurate systems, or efficient systems. The task is to build systems that remain accountable to the human mission of the institution even as they scale beyond ordinary human speed. Without that anchor, efficiency becomes a vanity. With it, intelligent systems become what they were meant to be: instruments of disciplined, ethical, and trustworthy enterprise action.

Conclusion: The Burden of Knowing

Algorithmic accountability is not a peripheral concern in the intelligent enterprise. It is one of the central burdens of leadership itself. Once an organization delegates action, inference, recommendation, or enforcement to intelligent systems, it also assumes a new obligation: the obligation to know. To know how the system reached its conclusions. To know where authority resides. To know which values have been translated into logic and which have been left behind as empty rhetoric. To know, above all, that speed does not dissolve responsibility.

This is what separates mature intelligent enterprises from merely ambitious ones. Immature organizations deploy systems and hope that performance will justify the architecture. Mature organizations build systems whose decisions can be explained, traced, challenged, and defended. They understand that autonomy without accountability is not innovation. It is exposure. They understand that every increase in machine agency must be matched by an increase in human clarity. And they understand that leadership cannot hide behind the complexity of its own machinery.

That is the deeper lesson of this chapter. The black box is no longer a defense. The liability gap is real. Explainability is no longer optional. Accountability must be structured across levels of autonomy. Ethics must be coded into the logic gates. Efficiency must remain anchored to mission. Together, these realities form a new standard for enterprise seriousness. The institution must be able to say not only that its systems are effective, but that they remain attributable, governable, and ethically bound under pressure.

Yet accountability, by itself, is still not enough. An organization may know who is responsible, preserve reasoning traces, and define escalation boundaries, but still fail if it has not addressed a more foundational problem: the quality of the data flowing into the system in the first place. A perfectly governed system can still produce flawed results if its inputs are stale, biased, incomplete, or strategically incoherent. In intelligent systems, bad judgment is often not born in the model. It is born much earlier, in the condition of the data itself.

That is where the discussion must go next.

If accountability governs what the system is answerable for, then data provenance governs what the system can know. The next chapter turns to that deeper layer of truth, trust, and architectural integrity. Because before an enterprise can trust what a system decides, it must first confront a more basic question: can it trust what the system has been taught to believe?

Part III: Technical Architectures for Leaders

7: The Hybrid Cloud Strategy

The Single Cloud Trap

In the early era of cloud migration, the prevailing logic was simple: go all in. Organizations chose a primary platform, committed to a single strategic provider, and moved as much of their digital estate as possible into one ecosystem. For a time, the approach was rational. It simplified procurement. It reduced the operational burden of supporting multiple architectures. It allowed teams to build deep platform expertise and benefit from tightly integrated services. Standardization created efficiency, and efficiency was often treated as the highest form of architectural maturity.

In 2026, that logic looks far less complete.

All in strategy has revealed a structural weakness that many organizations underestimated in the rush toward simplification. What appears operationally efficient in stable conditions can become a governance trap under pressure. When identity, data processing, AI services, compliance instrumentation, workflow automation, and operational resilience all depend too heavily on a single provider, the enterprise accumulates a dangerous concentration of dependency. Technical convenience begins to mask strategic fragility.

This is the single cloud trap.

The trap does not lie in using one cloud platform extensively. Many enterprises will and should continue to do so. The danger arises when the institution allows one provider to become the sole environment through which all critical intelligence, control, and execution must pass. At that point, the enterprise no longer has a cloud strategy. It has a dependency strategy. If the provider experiences a regional outage, a control plane disruption, a service limitation, a material pricing shift, or a change in model governance, privacy handling, or service terms, the organization's room to maneuver narrows dramatically. The issue is not only uptime. It is institutional sovereignty.

This matters even more in intelligent systems environments because modern enterprises increasingly rely on cloud providers not only for infrastructure, but for identity, governance integration, model access, observability, and orchestration. Microsoft continues to emphasize Entra ID Governance and Purview as cross organizational identity governance and data governance capabilities, while Azure OpenAI remains positioned as enterprise access to OpenAI models on Azure. AWS, by contrast, emphasizes Bedrock for foundation model access across providers and IAM for flexible identity and authorization controls. When these capabilities become deeply embedded in enterprise workflow, a single provider decision can have consequences far beyond infrastructure. It can affect governance posture, model choice, risk concentration, and operational continuity at once.

That is why the architect-leader must think beyond the algorithm and beyond the vendor narrative. To lead intelligent systems responsibly, leadership must also lead infrastructure. The question is no longer merely which platform is most convenient or most familiar. The question is how to design an environment that preserves resilience, bargaining power, control, and strategic flexibility while still allowing the enterprise to operate at scale.

This is where the hybrid cloud strategy becomes essential.

Hybrid cloud, properly understood, is not simply a matter of duplicating everything across two providers. Nor is it a symbolic hedge purchased for executive comfort. It is a deliberate architectural posture that reduces concentration risk while allowing the enterprise to use different platforms for what they do best. It is a strategy of balance rather than duplication. Its value lies not in novelty, but in optionality, resilience, and governance maturity.

For the architect-leader, the hybrid cloud is ultimately about preserving freedom of action. It ensures that no single outage, no single pricing lever, no single control change, and no single model governance decision can place the entire enterprise in a position of strategic captivity. In the intelligent enterprise, that is no longer a technical preference. It is a leadership obligation.

The Strategic Balance: Azure and AWS

For the architect-leader, hybrid cloud should never be treated as a simple exercise in redundancy. Its purpose is not to maintain two copies of every capability for their own sake. The real value of hybrid architecture lies in strategic differentiation, using each major platform according to its strongest architectural and governance advantages while avoiding unnecessary concentration of risk.

In high stakes enterprise environments, especially those shaped by governance, risk, compliance, identity control, and intelligent workflows, one of the most effective patterns is what may be called a *split plane architecture*. In this model, the organization separates the governance heavy control plane from the high scale processing plane. One environment is optimized for identity, policy, visibility, governance integration, and executive control. The other is optimized for compute elasticity, broad service flexibility, large scale processing, and model or workload diversity. The result is not duplication. It is purposeful distribution.

Microsoft Azure is often well suited to the control plane side of this architecture. Microsoft continues to position Entra ID Governance around identity governance, access process automation, and compliance-oriented control over who has access to what. Microsoft Purview is positioned as a unified portal for governing, protecting, and managing data across heterogeneous estates, including multicloud and hybrid environments. Azure OpenAI continues to be positioned around enterprise access to OpenAI models with the security promises of Azure. For enterprises already deeply invested in Microsoft identity, productivity, and compliance ecosystems, Azure can provide a strong foundation for governance-oriented functions, especially where role-based control, data governance, policy visibility, and office workflow integration matter most.

AWS is often compelling on the processing plane side. AWS continues to emphasize IAM as a flexible permissions framework, Bedrock as managed access to foundation models from multiple providers, and its broader cloud footprint for high scale compute and operational flexibility. AWS documentation also continues to stress Bedrock model access, IAM control, and policy-based authorization as central building blocks. That makes AWS especially attractive for workloads that demand broad infrastructure choice, large scale processing, data intensive pipelines, or model experimentation across multiple providers rather than a single model family.

This balance can be framed more clearly across several dimensions.

Dimension	**Microsoft Azure**	**Amazon Web Services**
Primary strategic strength	Governance oriented control plane	Elastic processing and service breadth
Identity and authorization	Strong enterprise identity posture through Entra ID Governance	Highly flexible IAM roles and policy models
AI orientation	Enterprise access to OpenAI models on Azure	Multi model access through Bedrock
Governance and data oversight	Unified governance and data protection emphasis through Purview	Strong configuration, policy, and operational monitoring capabilities
Common best fit	Identities, governance workflows,	Heavy processing, data pipelines, broad

Dimension	Microsoft Azure	Amazon Web Services
	compliance visibility, office integration	infrastructure patterns, model diversity

This framing should not be read as absolute. Both platforms are broad, and both can support governance, identity, AI, and large scale processing in serious enterprise environments. The point is not that Azure can only govern or that AWS can only process. The point is architectural emphasis. Leaders gain leverage when they stop asking which cloud should win and start asking which platform should carry which layer of responsibility.

A split plane hybrid model creates several strategic advantages. It reduces the blast radius of provider specific failure. It preserves optionality if service terms, cost structures, or governance models shift. It allows the enterprise to keep identity and policy anchored in one environment while distributing compute or model workloads across another. It also encourages cleaner thinking about architecture itself. Governance becomes a designed layer rather than an accidental byproduct of where the workload happened to land.

This is especially important for intelligent systems. If Azure is used to anchor identity, policy enforcement, governance visibility, and enterprise workflow controls, while AWS is used for scale intensive processing, data lake operations, or model diverse execution patterns, the enterprise can become both more secure and more adaptable. The governance layer remains disciplined. The processing layer remains powerful. The organization avoids the extremes of both fragmentation and over concentration.

That is the deeper promise of the hybrid cloud strategy. It is not about owning two clouds. It is about building one enterprise that is resilient enough to govern intelligence without becoming captive to a single platform's assumptions. For the architect-leader, that is not simply an infrastructure decision. It is an act of strategic design.

Interoperability: The Language of Portability

The greatest obstacle to a serious hybrid cloud strategy is not cost, nor even complexity in the abstract. It is vendor lock in. Every major provider benefits when an enterprise becomes so deeply entangled in proprietary services, interfaces, and operational assumptions that leaving becomes economically painful, technically disruptive, or strategically unrealistic. That is the hidden gravity of the cloud market. The longer an institution remains dependent on one provider's native patterns for identity, orchestration, data movement, observability, and AI services, the more difficult it becomes to preserve genuine architectural freedom.

For the architect-leader, this is not merely a procurement concern. It is a concern of governance. An enterprise that cannot move cannot negotiate effectively, cannot adapt quickly, and cannot preserve full control over the conditions under which its intelligent systems operate. Leadership authority weakens the moment infrastructure choices become irreversible. This is why hybrid cloud succeeds or fails on one principle above all others: portability.

Portability is the language of sovereignty in modern architecture. It allows the organization to treat workloads, agents, and workflows as enterprise assets first and hosting decisions second. Without portability, a company does not truly own its operating model. It merely rents access to it under increasingly provider specific terms. With portability, the enterprise regains strategic leverage. It can shift, replicate, fail over, negotiate, and redesign without rebuilding its entire intelligence layer every time the infrastructure context changes.

This is where agnostic technologies become decisive.

The first is *containerization*, most associated with Docker. Docker's own documentation describes containers as portable and consistent across environments, including local machines, data centers, and cloud providers. That portability matters because it allows intelligent agents and supporting services to be packaged in a way that is less tightly bound to the peculiarities of any single cloud environment. When an intelligent workflow is containerized, leadership is no longer managing a provider specific application in the narrowest sense. It is managing a portable enterprise capability that can be deployed where the institution's governance, resilience, and cost requirements make the most sense.

The second is *orchestration*, most associated with Kubernetes. Kubernetes documentation emphasizes production deployment across multiple zones for improved availability, and its broader architecture supports scheduling and managing workloads across distributed clusters. For the architect-leader, the value of orchestration is not simply operational efficiency. It is control. Kubernetes gives the enterprise a layer of workload management that sits above any individual machine and, to a meaningful degree, above provider specific infrastructure assumptions. That means the organization can manage agents, services, and containers through a consistent operational model even when those workloads are distributed across environments.

The third is *the gateway layer*, where technologies such as NGINX become valuable. NGINX documentation describes it as a reverse proxy and load balancer capable of distributing traffic across application servers, supporting performance, scalability, and fault tolerant configurations. In a hybrid cloud strategy, the gateway layer is more than a traffic manager. It is an architectural hinge. It enables the enterprise to route requests intelligently across cloud boundaries, enforce common ingress patterns, and abstract some of the complexity of distributed hosting from the applications and agents behind it.

Taken together, these technologies create the practical foundation for interoperability. They allow governance guardrails to travel with the workload rather than remaining trapped inside one provider's assumptions. The organization is no longer merely managing an Azure application or an AWS application. It is managing an enterprise intelligence asset whose runtime location can change without destroying its identity, policy logic, or operational purpose.

That is the deeper promise of portability. It transforms infrastructure from a place of confinement into a field of governed choice. For the architect-leader, that is one of the essential conditions of hybrid maturity.

Redundancy as a Governance Requirement

In regulated and mission critical environments, uptime is not merely an engineering metric. It is a requirement of governance. When a risk engine, onboarding workflow, compliance portal, or identity dependent intelligent system becomes unavailable, the organization does not experience only technical inconvenience. It experiences interrupted authority. Decisions stall. approvals fail. control signals disappear. auditability may degrade. In the intelligent enterprise, availability is inseparable from governability.

This is why redundancy must be understood as more than a resilience feature. It is a control requirement.

Traditional high availability strategies often focus on reducing downtime within a single provider by using multiple availability zones, redundant components, and failover design. Those remain important practices. Kubernetes guidance continues to emphasize spreading clusters across multiple zones to improve the likelihood that the cluster will continue functioning if one zone becomes unavailable. AWS similarly emphasizes that each Region is fully isolated and composed of multiple Availability Zones designed to isolate faults affecting resilience. But in the age of intelligent systems, the architect-leader must think beyond availability inside one provider's boundary. The real question is not only whether the workload survives a zonal event. It is whether the enterprise retains sovereign continuity when an entire provider, region, service dependency, or control plane assumption becomes stressed.

That is where hybrid cloud changes the equation.

By distributing critical portals, workflows, and intelligent services across distinct cloud backbones, the organization reduces the probability that a single provider level disruption will produce a total systemic blackout. The math is conceptually straightforward. If two independently governed environments each have their own probability of unavailability, then the probability of both being unavailable at the same time is far lower than the probability of either failing on its own. In simplified form, total availability can be approximated as:

$$Availability\_total = 1 - (Unavailability\_Azure \times Unavailability\_AWS)$$

This expression is a heuristic rather than a promise, and it works best when failures are not tightly correlated. But as a leadership concept, it captures an important truth. Redundancy across distinct infrastructures can materially improve continuity because the enterprise is no longer betting its entire operating posture on one fault domain.

The strategic shift here is subtle but profound. The organization moves from high availability to resilient sovereignty.

High availability asks whether the system remains up. Resilient sovereignty asks whether the institution remains in control even when something goes wrong. The first is technical. The second is architectural and executive. A system may be highly available within a single provider and still leave the enterprise strategically exposed if all identity, telemetry, policy enforcement, and model execution depend on the same cloud assumptions. By contrast, a hybrid design that separates these dependencies across multiple environments gives leadership room to maneuver under stress. The system is not merely harder to knock offline. It is harder to hold hostage.

For leaders, this becomes one of the most meaningful peace of mind metrics in the entire hybrid strategy. Redundancy is no longer just about uptime percentages or disaster recovery diagrams. It is about preserving the enterprise's ability to continue making decisions, enforcing controls, and sustaining intelligent workflows even when one part of the infrastructure landscape becomes unstable. That is the kind of resilience that boards, regulators, and executive teams increasingly care about, because it ties technical design directly to institutional continuity.

In that sense, redundancy is not excess. It is governance made concrete. It is the architectural expression of a serious enterprise refusing to place all of its authority, intelligence, and operational trust inside a single point of failure.

The Leader's Role in Cloud Negotiation

Architecture is never only a technical decision. It is a strategic decision with long term implications for resilience, bargaining power, governance, and institutional control. For that reason, the choice of cloud provider, or combination of providers, should never be delegated entirely to the engineering function. Engineering judgment is essential, but engineering alone will naturally tend to optimize for technical elegance, familiarity, speed of implementation, or ease of documentation. Those factors matter. They are not enough.

The architect-leader must bring a different lens. The real question is not simply which provider is easiest to deploy today. The real question is which architectural posture best protects the enterprise tomorrow. Leaders must think in terms of governance integrity, not merely implementation convenience. They must ask whether the chosen environment preserves institutional freedom, whether it strengthens resilience under stress, and whether it allows intelligent systems to remain portable, observable, and governable as the market and regulatory landscape change.

This is why cloud negotiation is not just a procurement activity. It is a leadership discipline. Every cloud commitment expresses assumptions about trust, dependency, data control, interoperability, and future leverage. Once those assumptions are embedded deeply enough, they become difficult to unwind. The role of leadership is to ensure that convenience in the present does not become captivity in the future.

That requires better questions.

A serious leader should ask the engineering and platform teams how quickly the organization could shift a critical inference engine, workflow, or intelligence service if a provider changed its data handling terms, service economics, or governance posture. The point of the question is not to force constant migration planning. It is to test whether the architecture still belongs to the enterprise or whether it has quietly become inseparable from the vendor.

A serious leader should ask whether identity management remains synchronized across environments in a way that preserves continuity of control. If the enterprise depends on federated identity, role governance, and real time authorization, then those functions cannot become fragmented by cloud boundaries. The question is not merely whether both environments can authenticate users. The question is whether the institution can preserve one coherent identity and accountability fabric across both.

A serious leader should also ask whether the centralized visibility layer can see the compliance state of one environment as clearly as it sees the other. A hybrid architecture is only mature if its governance layer is also hybrid in practice. If the portal can illuminate one side of the cloud estate while leaving the other in comparative shadow, then the organization has gained infrastructure diversity without achieving oversight coherence. That is not resilience. It is asymmetry disguised as maturity.

These questions reveal something deeper about leadership in technical environments. The executive does not need to dictate every architectural decision, but the executive must establish the criteria by which architecture will be judged. Those criteria must include portability, identity coherence, observability, redundancy, and governance transparency. Otherwise, the organization risks building an infrastructure that is technically impressive but strategically brittle.

This is the true role of the architect-leader in cloud negotiation. The leader ensures that cloud choice remains aligned with enterprise sovereignty. The leader insists that every provider decision be evaluated not only for capability, but for reversibility, resilience, and control. And the leader refuses to allow the future of the enterprise to be determined solely by whichever platform appears easiest in the moment.

In that sense, cloud negotiation is not about vendor preference. It is about preserving the institution's freedom to govern intelligence on its own terms.

Conclusion: The Resilient Foundation

The hybrid cloud is not a trend, nor merely an insurance policy against outage. It is the resilient foundation of the future ready enterprise. It provides the scale, flexibility, and processing diversity required for intelligent systems, while preserving the redundancy, portability, and architectural sovereignty required for systems integrity. In an age when enterprises increasingly depend on distributed intelligence to act, decide, and govern at machine speed, that combination is no longer optional. It is foundational.

That is the deeper lesson of this chapter. Single cloud concentration may offer short term simplicity, but simplicity purchased at the cost of resilience is often only delayed fragility. The hybrid cloud strategy offers a more mature path. It allows the enterprise to avoid strategic captivity, distribute risk intelligently, preserve bargaining power, and build infrastructure that can continue operating even when one provider, one region, or one service boundary becomes unstable. Most importantly, it enables the architect-leader to govern infrastructure as a strategic asset rather than inherit it as a technical constraint.

A strong hybrid strategy also reinforces one of the central arguments of this book: intelligence can never be separated from architecture. The quality of the system's decisions depends in part on the quality of the environment in which those decisions are hosted, routed, authenticated, and observed. Governance does not sit above infrastructure. It is embodied within it. Cloud design, identity design, observability design, and failover design are all part of leadership design in the intelligent enterprise.

Yet even the strongest cloud foundation cannot secure the enterprise by itself. A hybrid strategy may protect the broad operating environment, but the integrity of the system is still tested in its most vulnerable moments of interaction. Every intelligent workflow, every portal query, every governance trigger, and every automated handoff ultimately depends on one smaller and more fragile unit of trust: the session itself.

That is where the discussion must go next.

In the next chapter, the lens narrows from the macroscopic architecture of the cloud to the microscopic architecture of the network. We move from platform resilience to transactional integrity, and to one of the most vulnerable points in the intelligent enterprise: the session.

The Strategic Cloud Decision Matrix

To move beyond the algorithm, a leader must stop viewing the cloud as a commodity utility and start viewing it as a strategic decision. The choice between Azure, AWS, or a deliberately hybrid combination of both should never be reduced to the path of least resistance for the engineering team. Ease of deployment matters, but it is not the governing question. The governing question is which architecture best preserves governance integrity, operational resilience, and strategic freedom for the specific intelligent systems the enterprise intends to run.

This is the central leadership shift. Cloud selection is not merely an infrastructure matter. It is a design choice about control, dependency, observability, portability, and the future negotiating position of the institution. A provider decision shapes not only where workloads run, but how identity is governed, how data is protected, how AI services are consumed, how quickly the organization can change course, and how resilient the enterprise remains when one part of the environment becomes unstable.

For that reason, the architect-leader needs a decision framework rather than a platform preference. The matrix below is designed to evaluate cloud posture according to the demands of the 2026 landscape, where model choice, governance tooling, identity architecture, licensing economics, data gravity, and hybrid execution each shape the long-term sovereignty of the enterprise. Azure continues to emphasize Entra ID Governance, Purview, Arc, and Azure OpenAI as parts of a governance-oriented enterprise stack, while AWS continues to emphasize IAM, Bedrock, and its broader cloud flexibility for large scale and model diverse execution.

Strategic Cloud Decision Matrix, 2026 Edition

Selecting a cloud platform is no longer a purely technical procurement decision. In the intelligent enterprise, cloud architecture shapes identity control, governance visibility, AI flexibility, data gravity, resiliency, and long term bargaining power. For that reason, the choice between Microsoft Azure, Amazon Web Services, or a deliberately hybrid model should be evaluated through a leadership lens rather than left solely to engineering convenience.

The matrix below is designed to help the Architect-Leader assess cloud posture according to mission need, governance integrity, and operational resilience. It should not be used to declare a universal winner. Its purpose is to identify which platform is best suited for which layer of enterprise responsibility and where a hybrid approach creates the strongest strategic position.

Figure 7.1. Strategic Cloud Decision Matrix for the Intelligent Enterprise

Decision Factor	Lean Toward Microsoft Azure	Lean Toward Amazon Web Services	Leadership Impact
AI Strategy	Prioritizes deep integration with Microsoft's enterprise ecosystem and OpenAI based services.	Prioritizes broader model optionality and multi model flexibility.	Balances ecosystem synergy against protection from model lock in.
GRC and Compliance	Strong fit where unified governance, enterprise data	Strong fit where cloud native monitoring,	Determines the depth and resolution of the

Decision Factor	Lean Toward Microsoft Azure	Lean Toward Amazon Web Services	Leadership Impact
	oversight, and hybrid management are primary requirements.	flexible controls, and large-scale operational visibility are emphasized.	real time compliance environment.
Identity and Access	Best fit for enterprises already anchored in Entra ID or legacy Active Directory patterns.	Best fit for environments requiring highly customized IAM policies across distributed microservices.	Establishes the foundation of machine identity and access integrity.
Licensing and ROI	Advantageous where Microsoft enterprise licensing, Windows workloads, or SQL Server investments already dominate.	Advantageous where Linux heavy, cloud native, or variable compute workloads drive the operating model.	Shapes whether cloud spend behaves as leveraged enterprise alignment or elastic operational cost.
Data Gravity	Strong fit when institutional truth resides primarily in Microsoft aligned environments such as SharePoint, OneDrive, or SQL based systems.	Strong fit when raw and analytical data already resides in S3, Redshift, or adjacent AWS services.	Reduces latency, egress cost, and friction in intelligent workflows.
Hybrid Execution	Well suited when leadership must	Well suited when intelligence must	Determines the physical reach of

Decision Factor	Lean Toward Microsoft Azure	Lean Toward Amazon Web Services	Leadership Impact
	govern legacy and on premises environments through a unified management layer.	extend outward to edge or distributed operational environments.	the enterprise's leadership architecture.

Applying the Matrix

The value of the matrix lies in disciplined use. First, leaders should apply weighted scoring rather than assuming all categories carry equal importance. A compliance driven enterprise may weight governance and identity heavily, while an innovation driven enterprise may give greater emphasis to AI flexibility and data gravity. Second, the matrix should be used to test whether the organization's control plane and processing plane belong on the same provider or should be intentionally separated. In many mature environments, governance, identity, and workflow visibility are anchored on one platform while compute intensive workloads run on another. Third, every decision should be tested against exit feasibility. If a workload cannot be moved within a reasonable period because its data, logic, or governance structure is too deeply embedded in proprietary services, the enterprise has already begun to surrender architectural sovereignty.

A strong cloud strategy does not begin by asking which provider is more popular or easier to deploy. It begins by asking which architectural posture best preserves control, resilience, and future freedom of action.

The 90-Day Transition Roadmap

Siloed AI Project to Split-Plane Architecture

A hybrid strategy is only meaningful if it can be operationalized. For many organizations, the real challenge is not understanding the value of a split plane model in theory, but knowing how to move from a legacy, siloed AI deployment to a governed intelligent system without losing momentum. The purpose of this roadmap is to provide a structured ninety day path for that transition.

This roadmap is designed for enterprises beginning with a functional but weakly governed black box AI tool and moving toward a split plane architecture in which the Azure control plane governs identity, policy, and compliance visibility while AWS or a private data plane carries compute intensive processing. Throughout the transition, the objective is not merely technical migration. It is the preservation of continuous governance, so that the organization does not create new speed while sacrificing accountability.

The sequence is organized into three phases. Each phase builds on the one before it, moving from identity sovereignty to architectural separation and then to observable, automated assurance.

Phase	Timeframe	Strategic Objective	Core Actions	Leadership Outcome
Phase 1: Discovery and Identity Alignment	**Days 1–30**	Establish identity sovereignty	Inventory shadow AI, undocumented keys, and hard coded credentials;	The enterprise gains attributable control over

Phase	Timeframe	Strategic Objective	Core Actions	Leadership Outcome
		across the environment	map data flows; establish Entra ID as the identity source of truth; synchronize identities across Azure and AWS; replace generic API keys with unique machine identities	every human and machine actor in the system
Phase 2: Architectural Decoupling	**Days 31–60**	Separate governance logic from processing logic	Configure the Azure control plane; enable governance visibility through Purview and Arc or equivalent services; move compute intensive inference workloads to AWS or private clusters; deploy a gateway between planes to enforce GRC validation before output release	The enterprise shifts from a black box AI tool to a split plane governed architecture
Phase 3: Observability and	**Days 61–90**	Convert technical telemetry into	Integrate logs and telemetry into a workflow portal; test kill switch	Leadership gains real time clarity, lower

Phase	Timeframe	Strategic Objective	Core Actions	Leadership Outcome
Automated Assurance		actionable leadership visibility	protocols; simulate logic drift and breach conditions; reduce signal noise; train leadership on management by exception; complete a final systemic audit	exception latency, and operational confidence in the new architecture

Phase 1: Discovery and Identity Alignment, Days 1 to 30

The first month is about establishing identity sovereignty. No organization can govern an intelligent system if it cannot identify the actors within it, human or machine, or trace how data, access, and authority move across the environment. Before architecture can be split, control must be established at the level of identity.

During **Days 1 through 10**, the organization conducts a full inventory and mapping exercise. The legacy stack must be audited comprehensively, with special attention to shadow AI deployments, undocumented API keys, hard coded credentials, unmanaged service accounts, and any unofficial automation that may already be influencing enterprise workflow. This period is also used to map the current data flow from ingestion through inference and output. The purpose is not only technical discovery, but governance discovery. Leadership must understand where the black box actually begins and ends.

During **Days 11 through 20**, the focus shifts to identity synchronization. Azure Entra ID becomes the primary source of truth for enterprise identity and access governance. If the organization is operating across Azure and AWS, middleware such as Keycloak or a similar federating layer can be used where needed to preserve identity synchronization across both environments. The strategic goal is to ensure that the enterprise does not have fragmented trust domains or competing identity authorities. Without a unified identity posture, the later governance model will remain unstable.

During **Days 21 through 30**, machine identity is formalized. Generic API keys and shared credentials must be replaced with managed identities, IAM roles, or equivalent machine level credentials tied back to the central control plane. Every autonomous agent, service, and workflow component should now have its own unique and revocable machine identity. This is the point at which the organization begins moving from anonymous automation to attributable agency. From a leadership perspective, this is one of the most important transitions in the entire roadmap because it establishes the basis for later revocation, traceability, and forensic accountability.

Phase 2: Architectural Decoupling, Days 31 to 60

The second month is about the split itself. Once the organization has established identity discipline, it can begin separating governance logic from processing logic. The central purpose of this phase is to decouple control from execution so that the enterprise can gain both resilience and architectural clarity.

During **Days 31 through 40**, the Azure control plane is configured. Governance capabilities such as data labeling, policy visibility, and hybrid resource management are brought online through tools such as Microsoft Purview and Azure Arc, or their functional equivalents within the enterprise environment. The purpose of this period is to create the first live visibility layer, allowing leadership and governance teams to begin seeing resources that may reside in AWS or on premises through a more unified control surface. This is the beginning of real governance cohesion.

During **Days 41 through 50**, compute heavy inference workloads are moved to the data plane. In many cases this will mean AWS based services, private GPU clusters, or another scale-oriented execution environment. The critical requirement is that these processing resources remain accessible only through the machine identities and role boundaries established during Phase 1. The data plane must not become a shadow environment simply because it now carries the heavier workloads. It must remain subordinate to the control logic of the enterprise.

During **Days 51 through 60**, the organization deploys the governance gateway between the two planes. Whether implemented through NGINX, FastAPI, or another secure gateway pattern, this layer acts as the traffic control mechanism between processing and release. No data, inference result, or system response should move from the data plane to the user facing environment without passing through a governance validation checkpoint. This is where compliance ceases to be a retrospective review and becomes an architectural precondition. The gateway becomes the embodiment of safety by design.

Phase 3: Observability and Automated Assurance, Days 61 to 90

The final month is about clarity. Once the architecture has been separated and governance pathways have been established, the enterprise must make the system visible enough to lead. A split plane model without telemetry and actionable observability would still leave leadership dependent on assumptions rather than control.

During **Days 61 through 70**, real time telemetry is integrated into a centralized workflow portal. Audit logs, event streams, and governance signals from both Azure and AWS are connected into a common visibility environment. The objective is not merely to collect logs, but to ensure the portal can distinguish between ordinary operational success, emerging compliance drift, and true governance breach. This is the moment when raw activity begins to become leadership intelligence.

During **Days 71 through 80**, the kill switch protocol is tested. The organization should simulate logic drift, anomalous behavior, policy breaches, or security events in order to verify that the control plane can revoke an agent's identity, halt a workflow, or escalate an exception in real time. This testing is essential because a kill switch that exists only on paper is not a governance control. It is a hope. The point of this phase is to prove that institutional authority can still interrupt machine speed when necessary.

During **Days 81 through 90**, the environment is refined and handed over into operational use. The portal's signal to noise ratio should be optimized so that leadership can govern by exception rather than exhaustion. The leadership team should be trained on how to interpret the dashboard, distinguish operational issues from governance failures, and act on real time signals without overreacting to routine variance. The phase concludes with a final systemic audit to verify that the new architecture satisfies regulatory, security, and policy requirements and that the split plane model is functioning as a governed intelligent system rather than merely a distributed technical stack.

The 90-Day Success Metrics

The success of the transition should be measured through a small number of concrete milestones rather than broad claims of modernization.

Milestone	Success Indicator
Day 30	One hundred percent of AI agents and automated services have a unique, traceable machine identity.
Day 60	Compute intensive workloads are operating in the data plane while governance logic remains anchored in the Azure control plane.
Day 90	Average leadership latency for compliance exceptions has been reduced by more than seventy percent.

These milestones matter because they measure more than technical progress. They measure governability. By Day 30, the enterprise should know who and what is acting inside the system. By Day 60, it should know where governance lives and where processing lives. By Day 90, it should be able to prove that the new architecture has materially improved the speed at which leadership can see, interpret, and respond to risk.

That is the real purpose of the roadmap. It does not merely migrate workloads. It restores leadership authority over intelligent systems.

8: Securing the Session

The Invisible Handshake

If the hybrid cloud is the mansion of the modern enterprise, then the network session is its plumbing. It is rarely admired, seldom visible, and often ignored until something goes wrong. Yet it is through this hidden infrastructure that trust moves. Leaders often direct their attention toward the most visible points of security: passwords, multifactor authentication, biometric verification, privileged account approval, and the other mechanisms that protect what might be called the front door of the company. Those controls remain essential, but in an intelligent enterprise they no longer capture the primary theater of risk.

The reason is simple. Most consequential activity now occurs behind the scenes.

Autonomous agents call APIs. Orchestration layers query databases. Monitoring tools stream telemetry. Model services retrieve context from knowledge stores. Governance engines validate thresholds before action is released. Identity tokens are exchanged, refreshed, and verified continuously as systems move data across cloud boundaries, workflow layers, and trust domains. The enterprise is no longer secured only at the point where a human signs in. It must be secured in the countless invisible handshakes that occur after humans have disappeared from view.

A session is the temporal window in which two entities trust one another long enough to exchange information or authorize action. That may involve an AI agent in AWS querying a governance database in Azure, an orchestration service requesting access to a policy engine, or a workflow gateway passing validated data to an inference layer. For the duration of that session, authority is assumed, identity is accepted, and data is allowed to move. That brief interval may last milliseconds or persist much longer depending on the architecture, but its significance is the same. The session is the moment at which trust becomes operational.

That is why session security is not a secondary technical detail. It is one of the central control points of the intelligent enterprise.

If the trust embodied in a session is compromised, the rest of the governance architecture can be neutralized from within. It does not matter that the portal is well designed, that the workflow is elegant, or that the compliance logic is sophisticated if the session itself can be intercepted, hijacked, replayed, or spoofed. A poisoned session feeds poisoned data into the system. A stolen session token can grant illegitimate authority while appearing entirely routine. A manipulated handshake can cause one system to trust another that has not truly earned that trust. In such cases, real time compliance does not merely fail to protect the enterprise. It becomes dependent on corrupted assumptions.

This is the hidden danger of the intelligent enterprise. The more the organization automates, the more trust is delegated into machine level interactions that occur outside ordinary human perception. Leaders may believe they are governing the enterprise through policies, workflows, and dashboards, while the real struggle is unfolding in the invisible exchanges between systems. The front line of governance is no longer only the identity challenge at the front door. It is also the integrity of the session inside the walls.

For the architect-leader, this requires a change in perspective. Securing the session is not simply a networking problem for engineers to solve somewhere below the executive line of sight. It is a governance problem because every intelligent workflow ultimately depends on whether two systems can trust each other correctly, briefly, and only within the boundaries intended. The leader must therefore understand that the session is where architecture, identity, data integrity, and control all converge. It is where trust is either made real or rendered fraudulent.

To lead an intelligent system well is to recognize that the invisible handshake is often the most consequential handshake in the enterprise.

The Vulnerability of Machine-to-Machine Logic

Human sessions, while never simple, are relatively easier to conceptualize. A person authenticates, performs a task, and ends the interaction. Even when the user experience is complex, the pattern remains intelligible to ordinary governance logic. There is a recognizable actor, a visible point of entry, and often at least some chance that suspicious activity will be noticed by the person involved. Human sessions unfold at human speed and within human perception.

Machine to machine sessions are fundamentally different.

In intelligent systems environments, most critical interactions no longer depend on a person being present at the moment trust is established. Services authenticate to services. Agents request tokens from identity providers. APIs exchange credentials automatically. Workflow engines open sessions to retrieve, validate, and move data without ever presenting a login screen, a user prompt, or an obvious moment of awareness. Trust is created and consumed automatically, often at volumes and velocities no human observer could follow directly.

This introduces a different class of vulnerability.

First, machine-to-machine sessions are *high velocity*. Thousands of sessions may be initiated, validated, refreshed, and terminated within seconds. In such an environment, attack surface expands not only because there are more interactions, but because the pace of interaction reduces the time available for ordinary human scrutiny. What appears as a minor anomaly in one exchange can propagate rapidly when multiplied across machine speed workflows.

Second, machine to machine sessions are often *persistent*. Some agents maintain long lived sessions in order to stream telemetry, preserve context, reduce authentication friction, or sustain continuous service communication. Persistence is operationally useful, but it also creates opportunity for adversaries. The longer a trust relationship remains active, the greater the importance of ensuring that the session cannot be silently abused, replayed, or inherited by an unauthorized process.

Third, machine to machine sessions are often *invisible*. There is no human user to receive a suspicious login notification, question an unfamiliar access request, or feel that something about the interaction seems wrong. Machines do not get uneasy. They do not pause because an action feels out of place. They execute logic. If the trust relationship has been improperly established, the machine may continue behaving with perfect procedural confidence while serving a malicious or corrupted session context.

This invisibility is what makes the session such a prime target for systemic subversion. An attacker who compromises a front door credential may still need to navigate detection, user behavior, and explicit oversight. An attacker or failure condition that compromises machine level trust can sometimes move more quietly, because the affected interactions are already expected to be constant, fast, and largely unseen. A fraudulent request may look like routine telemetry. A stolen token may appear to be a valid machine identity. A compromised session may inherit legitimacy from the very controls that were meant to make automation possible.

For the architect-leader, the implication is clear. Security can no longer be framed primarily as perimeter defense. The front door still matters, but it no longer defines the whole risk landscape. In a world of autonomous systems, the security posture of the enterprise must extend inward to the logic of the session itself. The critical question becomes not only who may enter, but how systems continue to trust one another once they are already inside.

This is the move from perimeter security to session integrity.

Perimeter security asks whether the entity at the boundary should be allowed in. Session integrity asks whether the trust relationship inside the workflow remains valid, constrained, and uncompromised for every exchange that follows. Perimeter security is necessary, but insufficient. A strong front door does not protect an enterprise whose internal handshakes can be manipulated, inherited, or replayed without resistance.

That is why the session sits so close to the heart of governance. If a session can be trusted correctly, data moves cleanly, control signals remain legitimate, and intelligent systems can operate with confidence. If the session cannot be trusted, then everything built on top of it becomes suspect. The workflow may still run. The portal may still display green. The logs may still appear orderly. But the logic feeding the enterprise has already been compromised at the point where trust was supposed to begin.

That is the vulnerability of machine-to-machine logic. And that is why securing the session is not a technical footnote to intelligent systems leadership. It is one of its core disciplines.

The Three Horsemen of Session Risk

To govern intelligent systems responsibly, a leader does not need to become a packet level engineer. But leadership does require fluency in the dominant failure modes of session security. If the session is where trust becomes operational, then session failure is where system trust begins to collapse. In the age of intelligent systems, three threats stand above the rest: session hijacking, packet interception, and spoofing.

The first is *session hijacking*, the threat of lateral movement through stolen trust. In this scenario, the attacker does not necessarily need to steal a password or compromise a user at the front door. Instead, the attacker captures an active session token or otherwise takes over an authenticated session already in progress. Once that token is under adversarial control, the attacker can insert themselves into a stream of trust that the system already recognizes as legitimate. To the control plane, nothing may appear obviously wrong. The machine identity remains familiar. The traffic pattern may even resemble normal activity. Yet behind that apparent legitimacy, the attacker is now operating under the authority of a trusted agent. From there, the attacker may move laterally through the environment, query connected systems, extract sensitive data, or initiate downstream actions that inherit the credibility of the compromised session.

This is what makes session hijacking so dangerous in intelligent enterprises. The compromise occurs not by forcing entry, but by inheriting trust already granted. The system continues to believe it is communicating with the legitimate actor, and leadership may therefore receive no immediate signal that delegated authority has been subverted.

The second is *packet interception*, sometimes described as the intelligence leak. Intelligent systems are voracious consumers and producers of data. They exchange model inputs, governance signals, policy queries, telemetry, identity assertions, and operational context continuously. If these sessions are not protected by strong and modern cryptographic mechanisms, an adversary may be able to observe the traffic in transit. Even when the attacker does not alter the data, simple observation can itself be profoundly damaging. Strategy, intellectual property, internal logic, model prompts, control metadata, and workflow intent may all be exposed through the patterns and contents of those exchanges.

For the architect-leader, this means session security is not only about preventing sabotage. It is also about preventing silent strategic extraction. An organization may believe its systems are operating normally while an adversary is harvesting the intellectual and operational DNA of the enterprise in real time. That is not merely a technical breach. It is a governance and competitive breach.

The third is *spoofing*, the threat of poisoned truth. Spoofing occurs when an unauthorized entity successfully presents itself as a trusted agent, service, or system component. In a human environment, impersonation is dangerous enough. In an intelligent enterprise, it becomes even more serious because machine trust is often fast, automatic, and highly procedural. If a workflow portal receives a compliance report, a telemetry stream, or a validation result from a spoofed agent that appears legitimate, leadership may begin making decisions based on fabricated reality. The system reports that controls are healthy when they are failing. It reports that a workflow completed correctly when it was manipulated. It reports compliance when compromise is already underway.

This is one of the gravest possible failures of governance. It is not simply that the system is breached. It is that the enterprise is being governed through falsified signals. At that point, the portal becomes a mirror of deception rather than a surface of truth.

Taken together, these three threats form the dominant horsemen of session risk. Hijacking steals trust already granted. Packet interception leaks the intelligence moving through the trust channel. Spoofing corrupts the very identity of the entities participating in the exchange. Each threat attacks the enterprise at the point where machine speed depends on machine trust. And for the architect-leader, that means session security is not an isolated cybersecurity issue. It is one of the primary conditions of trustworthy governance.

The Cryptographic Anchor: mTLS and Zero Trust Sessions

If the session is the point where trust becomes operational, then the architect-leader must ask a central question: how is that trust anchored. The answer lies in moving beyond one-sided assumptions of legitimacy and toward a model of mutual cryptographic verification. In other words, the handshake itself must become defensible.

In traditional web security, standard TLS establishes a protected channel by allowing the server to prove its identity to the client. That remains a major security improvement over unencrypted communication, but it is not always sufficient for intelligent enterprise workflows where machine identities are constantly exchanging sensitive data and control signals. In these environments, it is not enough for the client to trust the server. The server must also trust the client. Each side must verify the other before meaningful action is allowed to proceed.

This is where *mutual TLS*, or *mTLS*, becomes so important. In an mTLS model, the agent proves its identity to the database, API, or service, and the service proves its identity back to the agent. Trust is not assumed in one direction. It is established in both directions through cryptographic proof. Every time a session is initiated, both parties must demonstrate that they are who they claim to be. This matters because it reduces the risk that a spoofed or unauthorized entity can simply step into a workflow and be accepted as legitimate.

For the architect-leader, mTLS is more than a protocol decision. It is an architectural principle. It expresses the idea that in intelligent systems, trust must be reciprocal, explicit, and continuously validated rather than casually inherited.

Yet secure identity exchange alone is not enough. Session duration must also be governed. This is why mature intelligent enterprises increasingly rely on *short lived, zero trust tokens* rather than long lived trust relationships that remain active for hours or days. The logic is simple. The longer a token or session remains valid, the more time an attacker has to exploit it if compromised. Long lived trust creates convenience, but it also creates opportunity for abuse.

Short lived tokens reduce that opportunity. Instead of allowing a session to persist indefinitely, the system requires trust to be refreshed frequently. A token may expire in minutes rather than hours. A new session may require a new validation path rather than relying on yesterday's legitimacy. This does not eliminate risk, but it narrows the attack window and makes persistent compromise more difficult to sustain.

A zero-trust session model goes even further. It begins with the assumption that no entity, internal or external, should be trusted merely because it already exists inside the environment. Each session must reestablish trust based on present conditions, not inherited location. The system asks, in effect, not who were you an hour ago, but who are you right now, under this set of conditions, for this particular exchange.

This is where *cryptographic nonces* also become important. A nonce is a random value used once during a session exchange. Its purpose is to ensure freshness. By incorporating a unique, one-time value into the handshake, the system helps prevent replay attacks, situations in which an attacker records a previous session exchange and attempts to play it back later as though it were a valid current interaction. The nonce ensures that an old conversation cannot simply be reused as proof of present legitimacy.

Taken together, mTLS, short lived tokens, and nonce based freshness checks create a far more defensible trust model for intelligent systems. They ensure that trust is mutual rather than one sided, temporary rather than casually persistent, and current rather than replayable. That is the cryptographic anchor of session integrity.

For leadership, the significance is profound. These mechanisms are not simply technical controls layered beneath strategy. They are the means by which the organization protects the truthfulness of its own internal exchanges. If the handshake can be trusted, then the workflow has a fighting chance to remain trustworthy. If the handshake cannot be trusted, then every downstream control, report, and automated decision stands on compromised ground.

That is why securing the session is not just about encryption. It is about preserving the authenticity of machine trust in a world where machine speed now shapes enterprise reality.

Leadership Mandate: Validating the Plumbing

A leader does not need to become a network engineer in order to govern a secure enterprise. But leadership does require the discipline to ask the right architectural questions. In intelligent systems environments, the executive task is not to configure every certificate or troubleshoot every handshake personally. The task is to ensure that the enterprise has built its trust channels on foundations strong enough to support the speed, autonomy, and consequence of modern machine activity.

That means leaders must learn to validate the plumbing.

Validating the plumbing begins with a shift in mindset. Network sessions can no longer be treated as an invisible technical layer beneath executive concern. They are part of the leadership architecture because they determine whether machine identities, workflow actions, governance triggers, and data flows remain trustworthy in motion. When a session fails, the consequences do not stay confined to the engineering bay. They rise immediately into the realm of governance, compliance, legal exposure, and institutional trust. For that reason, the architect-leader must know which questions expose whether the underlying trust model is mature or fragile.

One such question concerns the method of machine authentication. Are machine to machine sessions secured through mutual TLS, where both parties prove identity cryptographically, or are they still relying on static API keys that can be copied, replayed, or misused with far less resistance. The difference between those two approaches is not a detail of implementation. It is a difference in the integrity of the enterprise's internal trust model.

Another critical question concerns session duration. What is the time to live for machine session tokens. If a token remains valid for hours or days, then any compromise of that token creates an extended window of opportunity for misuse. If the organization has embraced short lived credentials and frequent reauthentication, then the attack window narrows significantly. The leader need not memorize the exact token standards for every service, but the leader must understand whether the architecture privileges convenience over bounded trust.

A third question concerns the speed of governance response. If a session is hijacked in one environment, can the control plane in another environment detect the anomaly and trigger revocation quickly enough to matter. It is not enough to know that a kill switch exists in theory. The organization must know whether the control architecture can identify abnormal machine behavior, correlate it across trust domains, and interrupt the compromised workflow in seconds rather than minutes or hours. At machine speed, delayed authority is often indistinguishable from absent authority.

These kinds of questions define the leadership mandate in technical systems governance. They do not require the executive to descend into packet captures or certificate chain debugging. They require the executive to insist that engineering architecture be explainable at the level of institutional risk. Leaders must know whether trust is mutual or assumed, whether session life is bounded or prolonged, and whether anomaly response is theoretical or operationally tested.

This is what it means to validate the plumbing. It is not an exercise in technical vanity. It is the disciplined refusal to allow invisible infrastructure to become an invisible source of strategic weakness. The architect-leader understands that the systems moving value through the enterprise must also move trust through the enterprise, and that trust must be protected at the point where it becomes active, exchange by exchange, session by session.

Conclusion: Integrity in Motion

Securing the session is ultimately about preserving the purity of organizational intent as it moves across the wire. Every intelligent workflow begins with purpose. A policy is defined. A threshold is set. A governance rule is encoded. A machine identity is granted conditional authority. But between intention and execution lies transport. The system's meaning must travel. If that movement can be intercepted, spoofed, replayed, or inherited illegitimately, then the integrity of the enterprise is no longer determined by its strategy alone. It is determined by the trustworthiness of its motion.

This is why session security is the microscopic foundation of the velocity of trust. At the macro level, leaders speak about governance, visibility, accountability, and resilience. At the micro level, those ideals survive or fail inside the handshake. When every session is cryptographically verified, every token is bounded, and every packet moves through a defensible trust model, the organization earns the right to let intelligent systems operate at extraordinary speed. Speed becomes governable because trust remains intact while the system is in motion.

That is the deeper leadership lesson of this chapter. Security in intelligent enterprises can no longer be understood only as a question of access at the perimeter. It is also a question of authenticity in transit. The architect-leader must care not only who enters the system, but how the system continues to verify itself once work begins. Governance that cannot travel securely is governance that will eventually be undermined by the very complexity it seeks to manage.

Yet understanding the plumbing is still only half of the technical burden of modern leadership. Even when sessions are secured and trust is preserved in motion, the intelligent enterprise still depends on something else: a common language that allows systems, services, policies, and workflows to speak to one another coherently. The executive who wishes to bridge the gap between the boardroom and the engineering bay must therefore understand not only how systems are protected, but how they are connected.

That is where the discussion must go next.

9: Python for Executives

The Lingua Franca of Intelligence

In earlier decades, a leader could manage a technical organization effectively while remaining at a comfortable distance from the details of software logic. It was often enough to understand the broad shape of the technology landscape. An executive knew what a database was, recognized the distinction between a front end and a back end, and had a general sense of how the budget was being allocated across infrastructure, security, and cloud services. That level of abstraction was sufficient because much of leadership could still be exercised through people, process, and finance without requiring direct engagement with the language of execution itself.

In the age of intelligent systems, that comfortable distance is beginning to disappear.

The reason is not that every executive must become an engineer. The reason is that modern enterprise logic is increasingly expressed in software rather than only in policy, process maps, or organizational charts. Intelligent systems do not merely support business decisions from the margins. They now participate directly in how data is validated, how workflows are routed, how policies are enforced, how thresholds are interpreted, and how machine mediated action unfolds at scale. In such an environment, leadership cannot remain entirely detached from the language in which those decisions are encoded.

If the network session is the plumbing of the organization, then Python is increasingly its logic. It is one of the primary languages through which modern intelligence is written, governed, and deployed. The scripts that validate machine identities, transform data, invoke models, enforce workflow checks, route exceptions, and connect cloud services often rely on Python or Python adjacent logic. From model orchestration in scale-oriented environments to governance scripts supporting enterprise control functions, Python has become one of the most common threads binding the intelligent enterprise together.

That reality gives Python a significance beyond technical convenience. It becomes a language of institutional intent. Inside the enterprise, strategy is eventually translated into systems. Systems are expressed through code. And increasingly, that code is written in a form that leaders can at least learn to inspect, interpret, and question. This is why Python matters so much for executives. Not because it is fashionable. Not because it is the only language that matters. But because it often sits at the point where business logic, governance logic, and machine logic converge.

To lead technical teams with precision in 2026 and beyond, an executive does not need to become a professional software engineer. That is not the standard. The standard is something more practical and more important. The leader must become *code literate*. That means being able to look at a script, a validation rule, a workflow condition, or a logic gate and understand enough of its structure to ask serious questions. It means being able to see whether the organization's stated intent appears to be reflected in the system's actual behavior. It means being able to recognize when a policy promise has or has not been translated into executable discipline.

This is one of the quiet but profound shifts of intelligent leadership. In earlier eras, leaders could govern largely by reading reports about systems. In the coming era, they must increasingly be able to read something closer to the systems themselves. Python becomes, for the architect-leader, not merely a programming language, but an executive interface to the logic of the enterprise.

The Read Only Leader

The objective for an executive is not to write one thousand lines of production code, refactor data pipelines, or compete with the engineering team on implementation details. The objective is something much more strategic: *read only leadership.*

Read only leadership means acquiring enough fluency to inspect logic without claiming to own the craft of software construction. It means being able to read code the way a financially literate executive reads a balance sheet or the way a legally informed executive reads a contract. The leader may not produce the artifact personally, but the leader can interpret its meaning, identify areas of concern, and ask questions that separate performance from illusion. In an intelligent enterprise, that ability becomes a serious source of governance power.

Python is especially well suited to this role because readability is one of its defining strengths. Unlike languages whose syntax is dense, heavily symbolic, or structurally obscure to non-specialists, Python was intentionally designed to be closer to structured English. Blocks of logic are visible. Conditions are usually explicit. Data movement is often easier to trace. Functions tend to declare their purpose more clearly than in many older or more syntactically compressed languages. For an executive, this makes Python one of the few technical languages that can realistically serve as an interpretive bridge between leadership intent and engineering implementation.

That readability has strategic consequences. When an engineering leader says that the system is designed to prioritize privacy, fairness, security, or risk control, a code literate executive no longer has to accept the statement purely as an article of faith. The executive can ask to see the validation script, the threshold logic, or the relevant workflow condition. The question is no longer only whether the team intended to build the safeguard. The question becomes whether the safeguard is actually present in executable form. If the script says that personally identifiable information is masked before it enters the inference pipeline, then that promise can be inspected. If the code includes a rule that escalates cases above a defined risk threshold, then that rule can be read. If the workflow claims that anomalous sessions trigger revocation, then the logic can be traced.

This does not mean the executive audits every script personally. It means the executive is no longer structurally excluded from the language in which critical promises are made real. That changes the balance of leadership. It allows trust to remain present without becoming naive. It supports a healthier executive posture: not suspicion, but verification.

The difference between legacy executive leadership and Python literate leadership is therefore not cosmetic. A legacy executive might ask whether the project is on time, whether the budget is stable, or whether the team believes the controls are functioning. Those questions remain important, but they stop short of the logic itself. A Python literate executive asks a different class of question. What is the actual logic gate for the risk threshold exception. Where does the system enforce the privacy rule. How is the model output validated before release. What condition causes the workflow to escalate to human review. These questions do not bypass management. They deepen it.

The contrast can be framed clearly.

The Legacy Executive	**The Python Literate Executive**
Asks whether the project is on time	Asks what logic governs the risk threshold exception
Relies primarily on PowerPoint status reports	Relies on telemetry, workflow evidence, and script level validation
Operates on “I trust my team”	Operates on “Trust, but verify the code”

The Legacy Executive	The Python Literate Executive
Understands at the level of high-level concepts	Understands at the level of functional logic and decision conditions

Read only leadership is not about technical vanity. It is about recovering proximity to the mechanisms through which the enterprise now acts. In intelligent systems environments, values, controls, thresholds, and strategies do not remain persuasive because they are spoken. They remain real because they are executed. The executive who can read enough of that execution to test its integrity holds a fundamentally stronger leadership position than the one who must always rely on translation.

That is the promise of Python literacy for the modern executive. It is not a demand that leaders become coders. It is an invitation for leaders to become interpreters of the logic that increasingly governs their institutions.

The Anatomy of an Automated Audit

One of the most powerful applications of Python in the intelligent enterprise is not glamorous model development or advanced algorithm design. It is the automation of governance itself. In practical terms, Python gives organizations a way to convert oversight from a slow, episodic, labor intensive activity into a repeatable, scalable, and near real time discipline. That is why it matters so much to the architect-leader.

Consider the problem of vendor security validation. An enterprise with five thousand vendors may need to review certificates, control attestations, encryption standards, expiration dates, and policy exceptions across a constantly changing supply chain. Under a manual model, such an audit may take weeks of human effort, and by the time the review is completed, the state of the environment may already have changed. Under an automated model, a Python script can ingest the relevant data, query the necessary sources, compare the results against enterprise thresholds, and produce a governed output in seconds. What once required periodic sampling can become continuous oversight.

This is where Python becomes strategically important for leadership. The executive value is not merely speed. The value is the ability to encode governance expectations into a repeatable logic structure.

First, Python allows leadership to define parameters with precision. In a manual environment, pass and fail conditions are often interpreted with some degree of inconsistency across people, teams, or review cycles. In an automated environment, those conditions must be made explicit. What constitutes a valid certificate. What date threshold triggers a warning. What missing field produces an automatic failure. What control deficiency requires escalation rather than remediation. These are not only technical questions. They are leadership decisions translated into executable standards. A code literate executive understands that defining the threshold is often more important than admiring the output.

Second, Python creates consistency at scale. The same logic that evaluates the first vendor evaluates the five thousandth vendor. That matters because fairness, repeatability, and defensibility in governance depend on uniform treatment under equivalent conditions. Human reviewers, however skilled, are affected by fatigue, local interpretation, and timing pressure. Automated logic reduces that variability. It does not eliminate the need for judgment in edge cases, but it does ensure that standard cases are handled against the same criteria every time. For leadership, that creates a far more stable foundation for trust.

Third, Python enables oversight to scale in time as well as volume. A manual audit might occur once a year. An automated audit can be executed hourly, daily, or whenever relevant data changes. This is one of the most profound shifts in governance maturity. Oversight is no longer tied to the pace of human review cycles. It becomes tied to the pace of system activity. An organization can move from asking whether it was compliant at some prior moment to asking whether it remains compliant now.

For the architect-leader, this changes the meaning of audit itself. The audit is no longer only a backward-looking inspection. It becomes a living operational check, capable of running continuously as part of the system's normal rhythm. Python is one of the mechanisms that makes that transition possible because it gives governance a language in which rules can be executed rather than merely described.

That is the true anatomy of an automated audit. It is not just a script that saves time. It is a governance instrument that translates policy into logic, logic into action, and action into scalable oversight.

Bridging the Communication Gap

One of the most persistent obstacles in technical organizations is not infrastructure, tooling, or budget. It is translation. Between executive leadership and engineering teams there is often a profound communication gap, and beneath that gap lies an even deeper respect gap.

Engineers frequently believe that leaders promise outcomes the technology cannot realistically deliver, compress complexity into slogans, and underestimate the effort required to build secure and reliable systems. Leaders, on the other hand, often believe that engineers overcomplicate solvable problems, hide behind jargon, and gold plate projects that should be moving faster. In many organizations, both perceptions contain a partial truth. The problem is not simply disagreement. The problem is that each side is often operating in a different language of reality.

This is where Python literacy becomes more important than many executives realize. The point is not that leaders must become members of the engineering guild. The point is that even modest code literacy changes the quality of the conversation. Once an executive can read basic logic, inspect a workflow condition, or understand the structure of a validation script, the discussion becomes more concrete. Abstraction gives way to evidence.

The shift is significant. A less technically literate leader may ask for a feature in broad commercial language and then grow frustrated when the implementation proves difficult. A more code literate leader is more likely to discuss the workflow itself, where the data enters, what conditions trigger escalation, what validation occurs before release, and where the true complexity sits. That difference matters because workflows are real. Features are often just labels.

The same is true in how problems are discussed. It is easy to complain about bugs in the abstract. It is more useful to discuss logic errors, exception handling failures, threshold misalignment, or edge cases the workflow did not anticipate. That language does more than sound more sophisticated. It changes the problem solving posture of the organization. It shifts the conversation from blame to structure.

And perhaps most importantly, Python literacy changes the way leaders approach the black box. A less confident executive may either fear the technical system and retreat from it or trust it too casually because it feels inaccessible. A more code literate executive does something better. The executive asks to see the inference pipeline, the validation rule, the threshold script, or the escalation logic. The system is no longer left in a realm of vague assurance. It becomes open to disciplined inquiry.

This has a cultural effect inside the organization. Engineers are far more likely to respect executive direction when they see that leadership is engaging the work at the level of logic rather than only at the level of presentation. Leaders are far more likely to trust engineering judgment when they can see how complexity is actually expressed in the system rather than hearing it only as explanation. The communication gap narrows because both parties are operating closer to a shared artifact: the workflow and the code that governs it.

That is why Python literacy can transform an executive from a consumer of technical services into a collaborative architect. The leader is no longer merely commissioning outcomes and waiting for translated updates. The leader can participate, at the right altitude, in the logic of construction itself. This does not erase the distinction between executive authority and engineering expertise. It strengthens it by making the relationship more honest, more precise, and more mutually intelligible.

In an intelligent enterprise, this is a serious advantage. Strategy increasingly succeeds or fails not on whether leaders can speak in visionary terms, but on whether they can ensure that technical execution remains aligned with the actual goals of the institution. Python literacy helps create that alignment because it gives leaders clearer sight into how promises become workflows, how workflows become systems, and how systems ultimately become the enterprise in motion.

The Ethics of the Script

There is a particular vanity in the pursuit of pure technical speed. Intelligent systems can process, classify, generate, and execute at extraordinary velocity. Python, as one of the primary languages of automation and enterprise logic, makes much of that possible. Yet speed alone is never the highest good. Toil without purpose remains a chasing after the wind, even when that toil is now performed by machines.

This is why Python matters not only as a technical language, but as a moral instrument. It is one of the means by which an organization can embed purpose into toil. In the intelligent enterprise, ethical commitments cannot remain safely confined to policy statements, annual training slides, or aspirational language in governance documents. If they are not translated into the logic of execution, they remain vulnerable to being overridden by convenience, efficiency, or local optimization.

Python gives leaders a pathway to prevent that drift. By understanding the structure of the code, even at a read-only level, executives can begin to verify whether the enterprise's values have been made operational. If the organization claims fairness in hiring algorithms, then that claim should be reflected in the validation logic, the threshold testing, the bias controls, and the escalation pathways embedded in the workflow. If the organization claims transparency in financial reporting, then that principle should appear in the scripts that validate inputs, preserve traceability, and prevent silent manipulation of outputs. If the organization claims privacy as a governing value, then the code should show where personally identifiable information is masked, restricted, or excluded from inappropriate inference paths.

This is where the architect leader proves seriousness. It is one thing to approve an ethical principle in the abstract. It is another to ensure that the principle survives translation into executable logic. The ethical standard is no longer merely something the company says. It becomes something the system is required to do, or prohibited from violating, in the ordinary course of operation.

For that reason, the ethics of the script should never be treated as a niche concern for compliance teams or technical reviewers alone. It is a central leadership responsibility. The question is not simply whether the code works. The question is whether the code works in service of the right ends. Does it reflect the institution's declared mission. Does it preserve fairness, transparency, privacy, and accountability where those values matter most. Does it reinforce human flourishing, or does it merely optimize throughput while leaving the moral burden unexamined.

In the age of intelligent systems, ethics must become executable. Python is one of the places where that execution becomes visible. The leader who can read enough of the script to verify that purpose has been coded into toil holds a fundamentally stronger position than the leader who must assume that values survived the translation from boardroom intention to machine action.

That is the deeper promise of code literacy. It does not simply make the executive more technically informed. It makes the executive more capable of ensuring that the enterprise remains morally coherent as it scales.

Conclusion: The End of Part III

With this chapter, Part III reaches its conclusion.

The journey through these technical architectures has moved deliberately from the broadest structural layer to the most intimate logic of execution. We began with the macroscopic view of the hybrid cloud, where leadership was asked to think about sovereignty, resilience, and the strategic design of infrastructure. We then moved inward to the network session, where trust had to be protected in motion, handshake by handshake, across the hidden plumbing of the enterprise. Finally, we arrived at Python, the readable logic through which governance, automation, and institutional purpose are often translated into working systems.

Taken together, these chapters provide more than technical exposure. They provide the blueprints of the intelligent enterprise. They show that leadership can no longer remain detached from architecture, because architecture is now one of the primary ways leadership is expressed. Clouds define resilience. Sessions define trust in transit. Scripts define operational logic. These are no longer remote technical matters. They are part of the executive burden of stewardship.

Yet even a perfectly designed system does not exist in isolation. It does not float above the people who build it, use it, question it, or fear it. Intelligent systems are always embedded in a human context. They are imagined by people, engineered by people, adopted by people, and judged by people. If they are not led carefully, they can easily become sources of alienation, mistrust, and institutional anxiety rather than instruments of clarity and capability.

That is why the next movement of the book must turn from architecture to humanity. The intelligent enterprise is not sustained by infrastructure alone. It must also address the emotional, cultural, and organizational realities that emerge when people confront systems growing more autonomous, more complex, and more consequential. Technology may be the machinery of the enterprise, but people retain its meaning.

Part IV begins there.

Reading Python Like a Leader

For the architect leader, Python literacy is not about writing production software from scratch. It is about learning to recognize the structural elements of code that reveal whether a system is governed, secure, and aligned with enterprise intent. An executive does not need to understand every library, every framework, or every implementation detail. The executive does need to know where policy appears in logic, where failure is handled, where accountability is recorded, and where trust can be broken silently.

In practice, this means learning to read code as a leadership artifact. A script is not just a technical object. It is a living expression of organizational priorities. It shows what the system permits, what it rejects, what it ignores, and what it records for later accountability. That is why a code literate leader can derive so much value from a small number of recurring patterns.

1. The If Then of Integrity: Conditional Logic

Conditional logic is where the policy manual becomes operational reality. Every serious governance, risk, and compliance requirement should appear somewhere as a conditional check. The logic may be simple or complex, but the principle is the same. The system must decide what happens when data, behavior, or risk conditions either meet or fail to meet enterprise standards.

What the executive should look for are the most recognizable Python decision structures: if, elif, and else.

This is where the leader asks the most important GRC question of all: what happens when the data does not meet our standards.

A simple example might look like this:

</> Python

```
# A simple Vendor Risk Gate
if vendor_risk_score > 75:
   trigger_executive_review(vendor_id) # The "Manual Intervention" gate
   stop_onboarding()
else:
   proceed_to_compliance_check() # The "Automated Assurance" path
```

This small block of code carries real governance meaning. It shows that the system does not treat all vendors equally. It enforces a threshold. It escalates high risk cases into human review. It prevents the workflow from continuing automatically when the risk score crosses the enterprise boundary.

For the architect leader, the key issue is never simply whether the code runs. The key issue is whether the threshold reflects institutional intent. Why is the threshold set at seventy-five. Should it be lower. Should different vendor categories use different thresholds. Is executive review always the right intervention point. In other words, conditional logic is where leadership can see whether policy has actually been translated into execution.

2. The Safety Catch: Exception Handling

In a high stakes environment, a system crash is never only a technical problem. It is also a governance problem because a crash can destroy visibility at the very moment oversight is most needed. That is why exception handling matters so much.

What the executive should look for are the core Python resilience structures: try, except, and finally.

These structures answer a crucial GRC question: *if a key control dependency fails, does the system stop safely and visibly, or does it continue in a dangerous blind state.*

A simple example might look like this:

</> Python

```python
try:
    verify_rsa_certificate(session_id)
except ConnectionError:
    log_critical_alert("GRC Database unreachable. Halting all
    handshakes.")
    halt_system() # The "Kill Switch"
```

This is good governance logic because it does not allow uncertainty to pass silently into execution. If the verification step fails because the GRC database is unreachable, the system does not pretend everything is fine. It logs the event, treats it as critical, and halts the process.

That is what graceful failure looks like in an intelligent enterprise. The system does not bypass the control simply because the control is unavailable. It stops in a way that preserves visibility and authority.

For the leader, this is one of the clearest places to test whether the engineering architecture reflects real governance seriousness. A system that fails safely can be trusted more than one that fails quietly.

3. The Paper Trail: Logging and Auditing

If an event is not logged, then from a governance standpoint it may as well never have happened. In the age of intelligent systems, logs are not just debugging artifacts. They are evidence. They support forensic reconstruction, legal defensibility, auditability, and executive clarity.

What the executive should look for are structured logging functions such as logging.info(), logging.warning(), and logging.critical().

The key GRC question is: *does this log entry tell me who acted, what happened, and on what basis it happened.*

A simple audit trail entry might look like this:

```python
# Audit Trail Entry
logging.info(
        f"AGENT_ID: {agent_name} | ACTION: Data_Ingestion |
        STATUS: Approved | BY: Policy_A2"
)
```

This is valuable because it preserves a minimum chain of institutional memory. It identifies the machine identity, the action taken, the status of that action, and the policy basis under which it was approved.

A leader does not need to read every log. But the leader should know whether the system is producing logs that can support governance. Good logging gives the organization the ability to reconstruct decisions after the fact. Poor logging forces the enterprise into speculation at precisely the moment when confidence, regulators, or legal counsel require evidence.

4. The API Handshake: Requests and Security

Python is one of the most common languages used to connect services across the hybrid cloud. Through libraries that make web calls, scripts, agents, and services are constantly sending data, requesting decisions, and invoking downstream workflows. This is where the application layer and the trust layer meet.

What the executive should look for are patterns such as requests.post(), secure certificate verification, and explicit authorization headers.

The GRC question is: *are we verifying the identity of the endpoint, or are we trusting the connection too casually.*

A strong example might look like this:

</> Python

```python
# The Secure Handshake
response = requests.post(
    url,
    json=data,
    verify="/path/to/cert.pem"
) # 'verify' must be a real path, not 'False'
```

This matters because a connection across clouds is never just a convenience layer. It is a trust decision. If the certificate is properly verified, the system is taking active steps to confirm it is speaking to the right endpoint. If verification is disabled, the organization may be exposing itself to interception or impersonation.

For the architect leader, this is one of the most important executive reading skills in technical code. If the handshake is not secured, then the rest of the workflow may be operating on compromised trust.

5. Data Validation: The Schema

Every intelligent system is vulnerable to malformed input, incomplete data, and deliberate poisoning. That is why data validation is not optional. Before data enters the workflow, the organization must establish what valid data actually looks like.

What the executive should look for are data schema definitions such as `class Policy(BaseModel):` and validation constraints such as `Field(...)`.

The GRC question is: *how is the system preventing bad data from corrupting its logic.*

A simple example might look like this:

</> Python

```python
class AccessRequest(BaseModel):
    user_id: str
    access_level: int = Field(gt=0, lt=5) # Ensures level is between 1
                                          # and 4 only
```

This is a small but powerful control. It ensures that the system will not accept just any access level value. It constrains the input to a defined and governable range.

For the architect leader, schema validation is one of the clearest examples of ethics and governance taking executable form. The system is not merely hoping the input is clean. It is enforcing structural discipline before the logic proceeds.

The Executive Red Flag Checklist

For all the value Python can bring to executive clarity, there are also patterns that should immediately trigger concern. A code literate leader does not need to understand every nuance of a script to notice when something is structurally wrong. Certain snippets are red flags because they reveal trust shortcuts, swallowed failures, or bypassed controls.

```
verify=False
```

This disables SSL certificate checking.

What it means: The system is trusting an endpoint without properly verifying its identity.

Why it matters: This creates exposure to man in the middle attacks and undermines the integrity of the session itself.

```
except: pass
```

This catches an error and then does nothing.

What it means: The system is swallowing failures instead of surfacing them.

Why it matters: Leadership loses visibility. The workflow may continue as though nothing is wrong, leaving the enterprise blind to real control failure.

```
HARDCODED_KEY = "..."
```

A secret or credential is written directly in the script.

What it means: A key is being embedded in code rather than retrieved securely from a managed secret store.

Why it matters: This is a major security weakness. Secrets should reside in controlled vaulting services, not in source code.

```
if True:
```

A logic gate is always open.

What it means: A developer may have bypassed a control or forced a path open for testing.

Why it matters: If this remains in production, the governance check may be effectively disabled even though the code appears to contain it.

Why This Matters to Leadership

The true value of Python literacy is not technical vanity. It is governance confidence. Once an executive can recognize conditional logic, exception handling, logging patterns, secure API calls, and validation schemas, the conversation with engineering changes. Claims can be tested. Thresholds can be discussed concretely. Policy promises can be examined in executable form.

That is the point of read only leadership. The leader does not need to build the script. The leader needs to understand enough of the script to know whether the enterprise's intent is actually present in the logic.

In the intelligent enterprise, that is no small advantage. It is one of the clearest ways a leader moves from trusting abstractions to governing reality.

Part IV: The Human Element in a Machine World

10: Human-in-the-Loop 2.0

The Approval Bottleneck

In the first wave of enterprise AI implementation, roughly between 2023 and 2024, the phrase **human in the loop** was often treated as a reassuring synonym for manual approval. The logic was straightforward and, at first glance, reasonable. The system would generate a recommendation, classify a case, draft an output, or propose an action, and a human would stand at the final gate to approve or reject it. This arrangement was widely understood as the ultimate safeguard. Whatever the black box produced, it would not act without human consent.

In the early stages of AI adoption, this model provided psychological comfort. It allowed leaders, boards, regulators, and operational teams to believe that human authority remained firmly in control. The machine could accelerate work, but the human would remain the final conscience of the workflow. In an era still learning to trust intelligent systems, that assurance mattered.

By 2026, however, the limitations of this first generation model have become increasingly clear.

In an environment shaped by agentic systems, continuous automation, and machine speed decision cycles, the old manual approval model no longer functions as a meaningful safety mechanism in many contexts. Instead, it has become one of the primary causes of organizational paralysis. If an intelligent system can process five thousand regulatory filings, vendor reviews, or workflow decisions in the time it takes a human to orient to the first screen, forcing a person to click approve on each individual case does not create real safety. It merely relocates friction to the narrowest point in the process.

The result is the approval bottleneck.

This bottleneck is not only inefficient. It is deceptive. On paper, the organization can still claim that human oversight exists. In practice, the human is no longer exercising judgment in a meaningful way. Volume overwhelms discernment. The pace of the system turns the human into a throughput constraint rather than a true governance mechanism. The workflow appears controlled because approval remains technically present, but the quality of that control deteriorates as the demands of repetition rise.

That deterioration produces a second and more subtle problem: **performance fatigue**.

When a human is asked to review hundreds of decisions per hour, the role inevitably degrades. Attention thins. Pattern recognition becomes shallow. Exceptions begin to look routine. The reviewer stops functioning as a leader or even as a careful evaluator and starts functioning as a rubber stamp. The mind adapts to volume by conserving energy, and in doing so, it abandons the very vigilance the approval model was meant to preserve. The safety net becomes an illusion because the ritual of review remains while the substance of review quietly disappears.

This is one of the central human problems of the intelligent enterprise. Systems can scale faster than human judgment can be meaningfully applied at the transaction level. If leaders respond by forcing humans to remain in every loop, they do not preserve control. They often destroy the return on investment of the system while simultaneously hollowing out the integrity of human oversight.

The lesson is now unavoidable. Human in the loop cannot continue to mean manual approval by default. That definition belongs to an earlier stage of AI maturity. It may still be appropriate in narrow, high consequence scenarios, but it cannot serve as the universal model for governing intelligent systems at scale.

To lead in 2026 and beyond, organizations must move to a more mature model.

They must move to **Human in the Loop 2.0**.

The Shift: From Operator to Architect of Exceptions

The defining shift in Human in the Loop 2.0 is simple in concept, but profound in consequence. The human is no longer positioned as a permanent operator inside the standard workflow. The human becomes the architect of exceptions.

This marks a fundamental change in how leadership understands intervention. In the earlier model, the human's role was to approve, reject, or validate each transaction as it passed through the system. In the newer model, the human's role is to determine where judgment is genuinely needed, define the conditions under which escalation should occur, and intervene when the workflow reaches the limits of delegated machine authority. The human no longer executes the process step by step. The human governs the process structurally.

That distinction matters because it restores the value of human cognition. Humans are not most useful when asked to repeat the same low variance approval task hundreds of times. Humans are most useful when confronting ambiguity, interpreting context, resolving conflict, exercising proportionality, or making decisions that require moral, strategic, or institutional judgment. In other words, the question is no longer whether a human can approve the task. The more serious question is whether the task contains the kind of uncertainty that actually requires human thought.

This is the core design principle of HITL 2.0. The workflow should be automated where the conditions are stable, bounded, and governable. Human cognition should be inserted where variance rises, context matters, or the consequences of ambiguity exceed what the system has been authorized to resolve on its own.

That change transforms the human role from reactive to proactive. In the old model, the human waits for the system to ask for permission. In the new model, the human defines the logic gates in advance. The human determines what confidence thresholds require escalation, what risk scores trigger manual review, what categories of exception deserve executive attention, and what boundaries the system must never cross without deliberate human reentry. This is a far more strategic use of leadership than repetitive approval ever was.

The contrast can be framed clearly:

Dimension	HITL 1.0, The Operator	HITL 2.0, The Architect
Human role	Approving every transaction	Managing high variance anomalies and exceptions
System interaction	Reactive, waiting for prompts	Proactive, defining logic gates and escalation paths
Primary value	Verification	Contextual judgment
Impact on speed	Linear, limited by human hours	Exponential, limited primarily by system logic

The importance of this shift extends beyond efficiency. It changes the dignity of human participation in intelligent systems. In the operator model, the human is often reduced to a procedural checkpoint. In the architect model, the human remains the source of judgment, meaning, and institutional boundary setting. This is not the removal of people from the system. It is the elevation of people to the place where they add the most value.

For the architect leader, this redesign is essential. The enterprise must stop confusing constant human presence with meaningful human control. True control does not come from forcing a person to touch every decision. It comes from designing a workflow in which machine speed is bounded by intelligently placed thresholds, and human expertise is reserved for the moments when it is actually irreplaceable.

That is the beginning of Human in the Loop 2.0. It is not a retreat from oversight. It is the maturation of oversight into a form capable of surviving scale.

Defining Meaningful Human Intervention

If Human in the Loop 2.0 is to function as more than a slogan, the architect leader must define what meaningful human intervention actually is. Without that clarity, organizations often fall back into one of two familiar errors. Either they place humans back into every transaction, recreating the approval bottleneck under a new name, or they remove humans so completely that the system loses the benefit of judgment precisely where judgment matters most.

Meaningful human intervention solves that problem by drawing a sharper distinction between review and contribution. In a high stakes governance, risk, and compliance environment, meaningful human intervention is not the act of checking work mechanically after the system has already formed a recommendation. It is the act of adding strategic context, ethical interpretation, or institutional judgment that the machine cannot provide on its own. The purpose of intervention is not to repeat the machine's logic at slower speed. It is to supply what the machine lacks.

This distinction is essential because intelligent systems are often strongest in structured, repeatable, rule bounded environments and weakest in conditions of ambiguity, consequence, or evolving intent. The architect leader must therefore define the zones in which human cognition is not optional, but mandatory.

The first is the *grey zone*, the zone of ambiguity. This is where the system's confidence falls below an acceptable threshold or where the input does not fit cleanly within existing templates, rules, or known decision patterns. A document may be legally unusual, a vendor submission may present a novel control structure, or a workflow may encounter a case that lies just outside the boundary of past experience. In these situations, the machine may still produce an answer, but confidence alone is not enough. The issue is not whether the system can respond. The issue is whether the response deserves institutional reliance. The human enters here not because the machine has stopped, but because ambiguity requires interpretation.

The second is the *high stakes zone*, the zone of impact. Some decisions are too consequential to be delegated entirely, regardless of how confident the system appears to be. A workflow may involve material legal exposure, major financial commitment, safety implications, regulatory consequence, or significant reputational risk. In such cases, confidence does not erase consequence. A system may be ninety nine percent certain and still be operating in a domain where the one percent failure case is unacceptable without human accountability. This is one of the most important principles of HITL 2.0. Human intervention is triggered not only by uncertainty, but by significance.

The third is the *drift zone*, the zone of evolution. Intelligent systems do not remain static simply because the code has not visibly changed. Data changes. workflows change. priorities change. incentives change. Over time, system behavior may begin to drift away from the ethical, strategic, or governance intent that originally justified its design. That drift may not be obvious in any single transaction. It often appears only through patterns. For that reason, meaningful human intervention must also include periodic review of the system's decision-making behavior at the pattern level. The human role here is not case by case approval, but institutional calibration. It is the discipline of asking whether the system is still becoming what the organization intended it to become.

Taken together, these three zones define the core of meaningful human intervention. Humans should enter where ambiguity requires interpretation, where impact demands accountability, and where drift threatens alignment. Outside those zones, the default should not be constant interruption. It should be governed by autonomy.

This is the mature form of oversight in the intelligent enterprise. It treats human cognition as precious rather than expendable. It reserves intervention for the places where human judgment is uniquely capable of adding value. And it prevents organizations from confusing constant human presence with meaningful human control.

Designing for Intervention by Exception

Once meaningful human intervention has been defined, the next leadership task is to design the workflow so that intervention occurs only when it is warranted. This is where Human in the Loop 2.0 becomes operational. Its technical manifestation is the *escalation protocol*.

In the older model, the system continuously paused to request permission. In the newer model, the system proceeds under delegated authority until a predefined logic gate is triggered. That is a profound redesign of trust. The machine does not beg for approval at every step. It acts within bounded authority until it reaches a threshold that requires human judgment to reenter the process.

This is what may be called *intervention by exception*.

Intervention by exception depends on carefully designed escalation gates inside the workflow portal. These gates are not random alerts or generic warnings. They are leadership decisions encoded into system logic. They define when ordinary autonomous operation becomes insufficient and when the system must stop, escalate, or request interpretive guidance. The architect leader's role is not to sit waiting for prompts all day. It is to design the conditions under which prompts should exist in the first place.

In a mature environment, this produces a deliberate asymmetry between routine activity and true exception handling.

The overwhelming majority of transactions should move through the system quietly. If the workflows are well designed, the data is clean, the policies are clear, and the trust thresholds are stable, then most activity should remain governed without demanding constant executive attention. This is the *quiet success* state. It is visible, but not disruptive. The leader sees it aggregated in green status bars, operational summaries, or confidence indicators within the workflow portal. It reassures without distracting.

The real value of the system appears when the remaining minority of cases become *noisy exceptions*. These are the transactions that cross a defined threshold of ambiguity, consequence, or drift. They trigger alerts not because something merely happened, but because something meaningful happened. When that alert appears, the system must do more than announce a problem. It must present the reasoning trace, the relevant context, the confidence conditions, the policy implications, and the decision options in a way that supports genuine human judgment.

A strong exception prompt therefore sounds less like a vague warning and more like a structured request for institutional interpretation. The system is not merely saying that something is wrong. It is saying, in effect, this vendor presents a nonstandard security posture, this document falls outside normal pattern confidence, or this transaction crosses a defined risk boundary. Here is the reasoning trace. Here is the relevant policy logic. Should the enterprise override, escalate, reject, or redesign the threshold itself.

That is the essence of intervention by exception. Human cognition is no longer wasted on predictable routine. It is concentrated where context matters most. This allows the enterprise to preserve the velocity of trust while ensuring that human judgment remains fully present at the edge of uncertainty and consequence.

The leadership advantage of this model is substantial. By focusing on the small percentage of decisions that truly require attention, the architect leader protects cognitive energy from dilution. The mind is not exhausted by endless low value approvals. It remains available for the rare but important moments where judgment, accountability, and institutional meaning must be applied.

This is one of the most important truths of Human in the Loop 2.0. Speed and oversight do not have to be enemies. They become enemies only when oversight is designed badly. When the workflow is built around intervention by exception, the organization gains something far more valuable than manual control. It gains disciplined control, the kind that preserves both velocity and seriousness.

Counteracting Automation Bias

The greatest danger in Human in the Loop 2.0 is not always insufficient human involvement. In many cases, it is uncritical human agreement. This is the problem of *automation bias*, the deeply human tendency to favor the recommendation of an automated system even when judgment, context, or common sense should prompt resistance.

Automation bias is dangerous precisely because it emerges in environments designed for trust. When a dashboard is clean, the portal is polished, and the system has performed well over time, leaders can begin to treat machine output not as an input to judgment, but as a substitute for judgment. Confidence in the system gradually hardens into deference. The leader stops interrogating the recommendation. The workflow continues. The anomaly becomes normalized. And the very structure designed to preserve human oversight begins to weaken from within.

This is one of the paradoxes of mature intelligent systems. The better the system performs, the greater the temptation to stop challenging it. A leader may still technically remain in the loop yet no longer function as a meaningful counterweight to machine logic. The dashboard is reviewed but not questioned. The exception is seen but not examined. The recommendation is approved, not because it has been judged superior, but because the system has earned enough habitual trust to silence scrutiny.

That is why Human in the Loop 2.0 must include not only escalation, but resistance. The human role is not merely to intervene when the system asks. It is also to remain intellectually active enough to challenge the system when agreement has become too automatic.

To counteract automation bias, the architect leader should introduce what may be called *adversarial intervention.* This means designing the oversight environment so that it occasionally tests, questions, or disrupts passive agreement. The goal is not to create distrust for its own sake. The goal is to preserve alertness, discernment, and the habit of active judgment.

One form of adversarial intervention is deliberate challenge through simulated error. At carefully chosen intervals, the system can present a controlled mock anomaly or edge case to test whether the human reviewer is still reading, interpreting, and applying judgment rather than simply approving by reflex. This is not unlike a fire drill for cognition. It trains the organization to remain capable of scrutiny under routine conditions before a real failure demands it.

Another form is reflective challenge generated by the system itself. If a leader repeatedly approves the same category of exception, the workflow portal can surface that pattern and ask a more strategic question. Have the assumptions behind these approvals been revisited. Has the risk context changed. Is the system detecting a normalized deviation that should no longer be treated as routine. In this way, the machine does not simply present decisions for approval. It becomes a disciplined counterpart that helps expose the human's own pattern of unexamined behavior.

This is one of the most important insights of the intelligent enterprise. Leadership in this age is not a one-way relationship in which humans merely supervise machine logic from above. At its best, it becomes a symmetrical conversation between human intuition and machine analysis. The machine offers scale, consistency, and pattern recognition. The human offers context, proportionality, ethical interpretation, and strategic sense making. Each should sharpen the other. Each should also guard against the other's characteristic failure modes.

For the architect leader, this means designing oversight environments that preserve productive tension. The human should not be reduced to a passive approver. The machine should not be treated as an oracle. A healthy Human in the Loop 2.0 model creates enough friction to prevent blind trust and enough structure to prevent chaos. That is how the organization keeps judgment alive at scale.

Conclusion: The Human Agent Partnership

Human in the Loop 2.0 is not an attempt to remove the human from the system. It is an effort to place the human at the highest point of leverage.

That is the defining shift of this chapter. The machine is allowed to absorb the toil of infinite scale, the repetitive, bounded, and high-volume work that can be executed with speed and consistency. The human, by contrast, is reserved for the work that remains irreducibly human: interpreting ambiguity, weighing consequence, calibrating drift, challenging assumptions, and providing the purpose that prevents efficiency from becoming empty motion. The result is not a diminished human role, but a more serious one.

This is the true promise of the human agent partnership. The intelligent system does not replace leadership. It changes the altitude at which leadership operates. Instead of spending cognitive energy on routine approval, the leader governs exceptions, defines escalation logic, preserves ethical alignment, and intervenes where the machine reaches the edge of delegated authority. That is not a retreat from responsibility. It is a refinement of responsibility into a form that can survive scale.

Yet every gain in efficiency creates a new tension. The more effectively the organization delegates toil into intelligent systems, the more urgently it must confront a deeper question. In a world increasingly optimized for speed, throughput, and decision scale, what happens to the human values that do not fit neatly into the logic of output. What happens to dignity, restraint, fairness, and moral seriousness when the machine's incentives pull relentlessly toward frictionless performance.

That is where the discussion must go next.

In the next chapter, the focus shifts from the design of human intervention to the larger moral tension at the center of the intelligent enterprise: the conflict between the machine's drive for efficiency and the leader's responsibility for ethics. That is the subject of ***The Ethics of Efficiency***.

The Decision Ready Escalation Principle

This chapter also establishes an important operating principle for the architecture that follows. In a Human in the Loop 2.0 environment, an escalation should never arrive as a vague notification alone. It should arrive as a *decision ready brief.*

When an intelligent system reaches a logic threshold it cannot resolve within its delegated authority, the workflow portal should not merely say that something happened. It should present the architect leader with a structured, high impact escalation interface: the context of the case, the reasoning trace, the risk implications, the available options, and the specific decision now required of human judgment.

That is how the gap between autonomous machine logic and human strategic oversight is properly bridged. The human does not reperform the machine's work. The human receives the machine's work in a form that supports serious judgment.

Executive Escalation Brief

Alert ID 8829

Priority: Critical
System Agent: GRC Vetting Alpha
Timestamp: 2026 03 29, 19:25 UTC

1. Signal Overview: What Happened

The system has paused the automated onboarding workflow for **Vendor: N Alpha Logistics**.

Primary action under review: RSA 4096 security handshake validation
Workflow status: Halted pending executive decision

This escalation indicates that the onboarding process did not fail because of a system outage or technical malfunction. The system halted because it encountered a security condition that exceeded its delegated authority for autonomous approval.

2. Logic Threshold: Why the Case Was Flagged

This escalation was triggered by a **logic variance** in the security protocol validation sequence.

Expected parameter: Valid SSL certificate anchored to a Tier 1 certificate authority root
Observed parameter: Certificate issued by an emerging market private certificate authority not currently included on the enterprise whitelist
Confidence score: 64 percent
Autonomous approval threshold: 95 percent

The system determined that the vendor's identity posture could not be validated with the degree of certainty required under the enterprise's zero trust session standard. As a result, the case was escalated rather than approved or rejected automatically.

3. Risk Quantization: What Is at Stake

Traditional governance models often describe risk through static labels such as low, medium, or high. In an intelligent enterprise, that language is no longer sufficient. Risk must be treated as a live, measurable variable calculated from current system telemetry, contextual exposure, and consequence weighting.

For this case, the system calculates risk using a real time expectancy model:

Risk Expectancy = (Probability of Compromise × Operational and Financial Impact) + Regulatory Exposure + Trust Degradation Factor

For this vendor event, the current calculation is as follows:

Probability of compromise: Moderate, estimated at 0.35 due to the nonstandard certificate authority and reduced verifiability of the trust chain
Operational and financial impact: High, because approval would permit access to Tier 2 supply chain telemetry and adjacent workflow data
Regulatory exposure: Elevated, because a nonconforming trust decision could weaken audit defensibility and violate established governance controls
Trust degradation factor: Material, because approving a nonstandard handshake without compensating control would weaken consistency in future session governance decisions

Composite quantified risk score: 8.2 out of 10

This score does not predict certainty of breach. It reflects the decision weighted expectancy of loss, exposure, and governance erosion if the system were to approve the vendor without additional control.

4. Reasoning Trace: How the System Reached This Position

The escalation includes the following explainability elements:

Feature importance:
The system assigned positive weight to the vendor's ten-year clean operating history at **plus 0.8**. However, the current

encryption handshake variance carried a negative weight of **minus 2.4**, making it the dominant factor in the final decision.

Counterfactual analysis:
If the vendor presented a certificate rooted in a recognized global certificate authority such as GlobalSign or DigiCert, the system would have approved the session autonomously.

Local interpretive logic:
The system concluded the following:
The vendor appears operationally legitimate, but the certificate path does not satisfy zero trust session validation requirements. I cannot verify the integrity of the private certificate authority with sufficient confidence to authorize automated onboarding.

This is not a generalized model judgment. It is the system's case specific explanation for why autonomy ended and human judgment became necessary.

5. Architectural Options: Decision Block

Option	Action	Systemic Impact
A. Override and Approve	Manually whitelist this specific certificate authority for this session	Highest workflow speed, but creates precedent risk and weakens trust consistency
B. Provisional Access	Grant 24 hour restricted access with sandboxed permissions	Balances operational continuity with bounded exposure and

Option	Action	Systemic Impact
	and heightened telemetry monitoring	reduced lateral movement risk
C. Reject and Re Route	Require a Tier 1 certificate or direct human vendor engagement before proceeding	Highest compliance integrity, lowest immediate operational speed

6. Architect's Note

This event represents *a **logic gap***, not a ***system failure***. The workflow halted precisely because the system recognized that the decision exceeded its confidence boundary and required human interpretation.

The value of this escalation is not merely that it stopped automation. The value is that it stopped automation with context. The reasoning trace, quantified risk, and decision options are now available in one view, allowing leadership to intervene strategically rather than procedurally.

Your decision in this case should not be understood as an isolated approval action. It will influence future logic weighting, trust calibration, and exception handling for this vendor class and comparable certificate patterns. In that sense, executive intervention is not merely operational. It is architectural.

Strategic Utility of the Escalation Brief

This template is designed to move the leader beyond rubber stamping and into strategic intervention. A weak escalation merely announces that something happened. A strong escalation presents the three elements required for judgment in one integrated view.

First, it provides the *why*, through the reasoning trace and threshold explanation.
Second, it provides the *stakes*, through quantified real time risk.
Third, it provides the *path forward*, through decision-repeated architectural options.

This matters because Human in the Loop 2.0 depends on preserving executive cognition for the small percentage of cases that truly define the enterprise's risk posture. The purpose of the escalation brief is therefore not to increase executive workload. It is to concentrate executive attention where it adds the most value.

Refining Risk Quantization

To strengthen this concept for the book, the Risk Quantization section should move decisively away from traditional red-yellow green heat map logic. Those models remain useful for broad communication, but they are too static for intelligent systems operating at machine speed. A modern control plane should treat risk as a dynamic variable derived from live telemetry rather than as a periodic categorical estimate.

A stronger conceptual framing would read like this:

Risk as a Dynamic Control Variable

In legacy governance environments, risk was often represented through static categories and periodic reviews. In intelligent systems, such representations are insufficient because the system acts continuously, context changes rapidly, and exposure accumulates in real time. Accordingly, risk must be treated not as a symbolic label, but as a measurable control variable.

The architect leader should therefore understand risk in terms of *expectancy value*, not mere presence. The relevant question is no longer simply whether risk exists, but how much expected exposure is generated by a given action under present conditions. This requires the control plane to compute risk dynamically using current telemetry, contextual sensitivity, control maturity, and probable downstream consequence.

A general form may be expressed as:

Risk Expectancy = Probability × Consequence × Exposure Duration × Trust Sensitivity

Where probability reflects the likelihood of compromise or failure, consequence reflects operational, financial, regulatory, or safety impact, exposure duration reflects how long the risky condition may persist before correction, and trust sensitivity reflects the degree to which the event could degrade broader institutional confidence or governance integrity.

Under this model, risk becomes actionable because it is continuously recalculated as conditions change. A vendor event, anomalous session, or compliance deviation is no longer treated as a static red box on a dashboard. It becomes a live decision variable that can trigger escalation, containment, provisional approval, or automated denial depending on the current state of the system.

That shift is foundational to real time governance. It aligns the language of risk with the operational reality of intelligent systems and gives leadership a more rigorous basis for intervention.

Refining the Math: The Systemic Risk Equation

In a Human in the Loop 2.0 environment, escalation cannot rest on intuition alone. If the enterprise is going to interrupt machine speed and elevate a case to human judgment, it must do so on a disciplined basis. That is why the escalation brief should rely on a refined systemic risk equation, one that draws conceptually from the FAIR tradition of information risk analysis but adapts it to the pace, autonomy, and telemetry rich conditions of intelligent systems.

At the center of this model is the idea that risk is not static. It accumulates over time, changes as system conditions change, and is either amplified or suppressed by the quality of governance and observability surrounding the event. In that sense, systemic risk is best understood not as a fixed score, but as a dynamic quantity unfolding across a decision interval.

A useful formulation is:

R_sys = ∫ from t_0 to t□ of ((f(T,V) × L) / (G × O)) dt

This equation expresses systemic risk as the cumulative risk carried by the enterprise over a defined period of time. It recognizes that risk rises when threat and vulnerability combine to create credible loss exposure, and that this exposure is reduced when governance efficacy and observability are strong.

The Variables Defined

f(T,V): Loss Event Frequency

This term represents the interaction between *Threat* and *Vulnerability*. Threat refers to the probability of an adversary, control failure, logic error, or other harmful event. Vulnerability refers to the weakness currently present in the environment that would allow that threat to produce meaningful harm. In practical terms, threat is the force pressing against the system, and vulnerability is the weakness that gives that force a place to enter. A legacy RSA 1024 handshake, an untrusted certificate authority, or an over permissive API session would all increase vulnerability immediately.

L: Magnitude of Loss

This is the blast radius of the event if it is mishandled or wrongly approved. It includes direct financial cost, legal or regulatory exposure, operational disruption, reputational damage, and secondary institutional loss such as weakened trust in governance. In a modern enterprise, magnitude of loss should never be reduced to dollars alone. It must also include the effects of broader systemic degradation.

G: Governance Efficacy

This represents the strength of the enterprise's guardrails.

Governance efficacy rises when escalation logic is mature, kill switches are functional, policy gates are embedded in workflow, and exception handling remains disciplined. A well-designed control plane with tested containment capability increases G and therefore reduces systemic risk. Weak or symbolic controls decrease G and allow the same threat condition to produce far greater exposure.

O: Observability

This is the clarity factor. Observability reflects how quickly and accurately the organization can detect, interpret, and respond to the event. High observability does not eliminate threat, but it shortens the duration over which risk can accumulate by making anomalies visible before they become systemic failures. In that sense, observability does not merely inform leadership. It changes the mathematics of exposure.

Why This Matters for the Architect Leader

The first reason this model matters is that it helps move governance from subjectivity to disciplined objectivity. Traditional GRC often relies heavily on expert judgment, which has value but is slow, inconsistent, and vulnerable to bias. A telemetry driven risk model is different. If the control plane observes that an API session is using a legacy RSA 1024 handshake instead of the required RSA 4096 standard, the vulnerability term rises immediately. The resulting increase in risk is not primarily a matter of opinion. It is a measurable consequence of the current architecture.

The second reason it matters is that it justifies intervention. In a Human in the Loop 2.0 model, escalation must be more than a procedural reflex. It must be a defensible decision. A quantified score, whether expressed as a normalized value such as 8.2 out of 10 or as a threshold crossing within the control plane, tells the leader why this case deserves cognitive attention. It explains that the interruption is not caused by trivial variance, but by a material combination of threat, vulnerability, and consequence significant enough to justify slowing the workflow and reintroducing human judgment.

The third reason it matters is that it allows the enterprise to demonstrate the return on governance itself. This is where mathematics becomes strategically powerful. If the organization improves observability through a stronger workflow portal, the O term increases. If it implements more effective kill switch logic or tighter escalation pathways, the G term increases. In both cases, residual systemic risk declines. The leader can therefore show that governance is not merely defensive overhead. It is a measurable reduction in exposure and a preservation of enterprise capital, legitimacy, and continuity.

A Simpler Executive Interpretation

For all its rigor, the equation should also be understandable at the executive level. Put simply, systemic risk rises when harmful events are more likely, the blast radius is larger, and the enterprise is weak in its controls or visibility. Systemic risk falls when governance is strong, observability is high, and the organization can detect and contain dangerous conditions quickly.

This means that the architect-leader does not need to become a mathematician. The leader must understand the directional logic of the equation. If vulnerability spikes, risk rises. If governance maturity improves, risk falls. If observability strengthens, risk duration shrinks. The model becomes a tool for disciplined prioritization rather than abstract technical display.

The Vanity of Precision

There is, however, an important warning here. Quantification is powerful, but it can also invite a false sense of mastery. There is a vanity in seeking perfect numbers, as though risk could be reduced to a third decimal point and thereby fully controlled. That is not the purpose of this model.

The architect leader is not searching for mathematical perfection. The leader is searching for *order of magnitude* clarity.

The point of quantization is prioritization. It helps the enterprise determine when the silent handover from human authority to machine execution should continue uninterrupted and when it must stop. It provides a disciplined basis for deciding which events deserve ordinary automation, which deserve heightened monitoring, and which deserve the uniquely human gift of contextual judgment.

That is the true value of the systemic risk equation. It does not eliminate uncertainty. It structures uncertainty well enough that leadership can govern it in real time.

Figure 10.2. Dynamic Systemic Risk in Human in the Loop 2.0

R_sys = ∫ from t_0 to t□ of ((f(T,V) × L) / (G × O)) dt

Where:

- **f(T,V)** represents the interaction of threat and vulnerability, or the frequency with which a loss event becomes plausible under current conditions.
- **L** represents the magnitude of potential loss, including financial, legal, operational, and reputational consequences.
- **G** represents governance efficacy, or the strength of the enterprise's guardrails, intervention logic, and containment controls.
- **O** represents observability, or the degree to which the enterprise can detect, interpret, and respond to the event before it becomes systemic.

Interpretive principle:
Systemic risk increases when threat, vulnerability, and loss magnitude rise. Systemic risk decreases when governance efficacy and observability improve.

11: The Ethics of Efficiency

The Replicator Paradox

In science fiction, the matter replicator has long stood as one of the great symbols of technological triumph. It represents abundance without labor, creation without scarcity, and production detached almost entirely from physical limitation. A machine can produce a cup of tea, a tool, or a complex component seemingly out of nothing, on demand, at negligible incremental cost. For generations of industrial thinking, this vision carried enormous appeal. It embodied the dream that productivity might one day escape the stubborn constraints of time, effort, and material friction.

In 2026, the enterprise has encountered the digital equivalent of that dream.

Intelligent systems now generate code, legal drafts, policy summaries, research outputs, design concepts, reports, and strategic analyses at a scale and speed that would have seemed implausible only a few years ago. What once required teams of specialists working over days or weeks can now be produced in minutes, sometimes seconds. The replicator has not arrived in physical form, but it has arrived in logic. The organization can now manufacture digital output at a pace that increasingly resembles abundance without labor.

Yet that achievement has exposed a paradox at the heart of intelligent enterprise life. When efficiency approaches infinity, the value of output does not necessarily rise with it. In many contexts, it begins to collapse.

This is the replicator paradox. The easier it becomes to produce something, the harder it becomes to guarantee that the thing produced is worth producing. Volume rises. Friction falls. Marginal cost approaches zero. But meaning, discernment, and strategic value do not automatically scale alongside output. In fact, they often weaken under the pressure of abundance. The enterprise finds itself awash in generated material while becoming less certain about significance. It can create more than ever before, yet struggle more intensely with the question of what deserves to exist, what deserves to be trusted, and what serves a purpose larger than the machine's own productive capacity.

This is why the challenge facing the architect leader has changed so fundamentally. The central question is no longer how to do more. Intelligent systems have already answered that question with remarkable force. The more serious question is why the enterprise is doing what it is doing at all. What mission is being served. What human purpose is being advanced. What form of value is being created that remains meaningful once speed, scale, and automation have removed so much of the old friction.

This is where ethics enters the conversation with full seriousness. Ethics in the intelligent enterprise is not merely about avoiding scandal, bias, or regulatory failure. It is also about resisting the drift toward purposeless productivity. The machine is naturally oriented toward output. It is designed to continue, extend, optimize, and scale. Human leadership must therefore ask the countervailing question. Toward what end. In whose service. At what cost to meaning, proportionality, or human flourishing.

The replicator metaphor is helpful precisely because it exposes the temptation so clearly. The ability to create at scale can easily seduce institutions into believing that creation itself is the justification. But in enterprise life, as in moral life, production is never self justifying. Output without purpose is not progress. It is activity untethered from reason. The architect leader must therefore become not only a governor of intelligent systems, but a guardian of institutional purpose in an age where output has become dangerously cheap.

The Fallacy of Infinite Scale

One of the most persistent errors in modern enterprise thinking is the assumption that if a modest gain in efficiency is beneficial, then limitless efficiency must be ideal. This assumption is rarely stated so bluntly, but it drives much of the enthusiasm surrounding intelligent systems. If a workflow can be accelerated, accelerate it. If a decision can be automated, automate it. If a process can be scaled without additional labor, scale it. Behind these instincts lies a powerful but flawed idea: that efficiency is self validating.

It is not.

Efficiency is a means. It has never been an end. It is valuable only insofar as it serves something more fundamental than itself. In healthy institutions, efficiency should support clarity, mission, stewardship, trust, service quality, resilience, or the wise use of human effort. When efficiency becomes detached from those higher purposes, it begins to distort decision making. The enterprise starts optimizing what is easiest to measure rather than what is most worth protecting. Throughput takes precedence over judgment. Friction is eliminated even where friction once served as a moral or strategic safeguard. The machine's preference for uninterrupted flow begins to override the human need for reflection, proportionality, and exception handling.

This is the fallacy of infinite scale.

The fallacy appears whenever leaders assume that the removal of all friction is automatically a sign of advancement. In reality, some forms of friction are not waste. They are safeguards. They are the places where the organization pauses to consider consequence, ambiguity, fairness, safety, or institutional legitimacy. The goal of intelligent leadership is not to eliminate all friction indiscriminately. It is to distinguish between wasteful friction and meaningful friction, between delay that impedes the mission and deliberation that protects it.

This is particularly important in governance, risk, and compliance environments. A system may automate a workflow so completely that it removes every visible point of human interruption. On one level, this may look like the highest form of maturity. The process is faster, cleaner, and more efficient. But if that same workflow loses the ability to recognize a rare ethical anomaly, a black swan event, or a context specific risk that was never encoded into the standard logic, then the gain in efficiency is not neutral. It has purchased speed at the cost of adaptive judgment.

That is not true efficiency. It is high velocity risk.

This is one of the hardest lessons for modern enterprises to learn because the failure may not appear immediately. The system may perform brilliantly for a long period. Metrics may improve. Cycle time may collapse. Leadership may celebrate the elimination of delay. Yet hidden inside that optimization is a dangerous brittleness. The workflow has become so smooth that it can no longer slow itself intelligently when the unusual, the ambiguous, or the morally significant enters the process. At that point, efficiency ceases to be a servant of the mission and becomes a threat to it.

The architect leader must therefore resist the seduction of pure scale. The purpose of intelligent systems is not to maximize output under every condition. The purpose is to extend the institution's capacity while preserving its humanity, its accountability, and its ability to respond wisely when the unexpected occurs. That means asking a harder question than how fast can this run. It means asking what kind of risk is created when nothing meaningful is left in the system to interrupt the machine's momentum.

This is where ethics and architecture meet. The more powerful the system becomes, the more important it is to encode not just speed, but restraint. Not just throughput, but judgment. Not just automation, but the capacity to stop, examine, and redirect when the enterprise is approaching decisions that exceed the machine's rightful authority.

Infinite scale is therefore not the highest ideal of the intelligent enterprise. Wise scale is. And wise scale always knows what it is for.

The Vanity of the Metric

There is an old warning in ancient wisdom that speaks with surprising force to the age of intelligent systems: toil without purpose is a chasing after the wind. In the modern enterprise, this warning appears in a new form. It appears as the **vanity of the metric**.

The vanity of the metric emerges when organizations begin mistaking measurable performance for meaningful value. Because intelligent systems can optimize at extraordinary speed, leaders are increasingly tempted to judge success by what the system can most easily count. Throughput rises. Latency falls. cost per transaction shrinks. Compliance checks complete faster. Reports are generated at scale.

Dashboards fill with evidence of motion. Yet none of these indicators, impressive as they may be, can answer the deeper question of whether the enterprise is actually moving in the right direction.

This is where metrics become dangerous. Metrics are indispensable, but they are never morally neutral. Every metric privileges a certain definition of success. Every optimization implies a hierarchy of values. If the organization rewards only the speed of compliance workflows, it may gradually begin optimizing for the appearance of compliance rather than the substance of it. If it rewards only profit maximization, it may begin extracting value in ways that erode trust, weaken resilience, or damage the very ecosystem on which long term success depends. The machine does not distinguish automatically between what is measurable and what is worthy. That distinction remains the burden of leadership.

This is why the vanity of the metric is not merely a technical risk. It is a philosophical one. A system can become extraordinarily effective at optimizing the wrong thing. It can produce compliance theater instead of compliance integrity. It can generate profit acceleration instead of sustainable value. It can reward surface level signals of success while quietly hollowing out the mission the organization exists to serve. Under those conditions, the enterprise may still look efficient from the outside, but its internal logic has begun to drift away from its purpose.

The problem becomes especially acute when leadership itself is judged primarily by output metrics. If the executive is rewarded only for the speed of the replicator, then the organization will naturally learn to privilege production over discernment. The system will run faster, but the institution may become less wise. It may stop asking whether the workflow still deserves to operate in its current form. It may lose the courage to pause, question, or interrupt the machine when the metrics are still green but the moral logic is beginning to fail.

That is what it means to lead a ghost ship. The machinery is in motion. The signals look healthy. The vessel appears efficient. But the deeper animating presence of judgment, mission, and human purpose has begun to disappear. At that point, leadership is no longer governing the system. It is being governed by the metrics the system happens to reward.

True leadership requires a harder discipline. It requires the courage to slow the system down when speed threatens meaning. It requires the willingness to ask not only whether the metrics are improving, but whether the metrics still deserve authority over the enterprise's decisions. And it requires the moral seriousness to recognize that some of the most important outcomes in institutional life, trust, dignity, legitimacy, and human flourishing, cannot be reduced fully to a dashboard without being diminished in the process.

The vanity of the metric, then, is not the existence of measurement. It is the illusion that measurement alone is enough.

Human Centric Values in a Machine World

To lead beyond the algorithm, human values cannot remain external commentary on machine activity. They must become part of the operating logic of the enterprise itself. This is the decisive shift from *efficiency* to *efficacy*.

Efficiency asks how to maximize output with minimum input. It is a legitimate and often necessary concern. Organizations must steward resources, reduce waste, and improve the pace and reliability of execution. But efficiency alone does not tell the institution whether its actions are serving the mission. It tells the institution how quickly and cheaply it is moving, not whether it is moving wisely.

Efficacy asks a different question. It asks whether the system is producing the right kind of impact for the purpose the enterprise exists to fulfill. It is concerned not merely with output, but with consequence. Not merely with performance, but with worth. Efficacy reintroduces judgment into a system otherwise tempted to optimize endlessly for frictionless production.

This difference can be framed clearly.

The Efficiency Mindset, Machine Logic	**The Efficacy Mindset, Human Logic**
Goal: Maximum output for minimum input	Goal: Maximum mission aligned impact
Metric: Throughput, latency, cost per token	Metric: Trust, integrity, human flourishing
Failure: A crash, delay, or logic error	Failure: An ethical breach or loss of purpose
Core question: Can we automate this	Core question: Should we automate this

This contrast is not meant to romanticize inefficiency or reject automation. The issue is not whether systems should become faster or more capable. The issue is what values govern the direction of that capability. A machine naturally privileges optimization because optimization is what it is built to do. A human centered enterprise must therefore provide the counterweight. It must ensure that trust, integrity, dignity, fairness, and long-term mission are not displaced by the easier language of throughput and cost reduction.

That is why human centric values must be hard coded into enterprise logic. They cannot remain only aspirational ideals repeated in policy manuals or annual statements of principle. If the organization claims to value integrity, then workflows must preserve traceability and accountability even when doing so adds friction. If it claims to value fairness, then systems must include mechanisms for bias review, contextual override, and exception analysis. If it claims to value human flourishing, then automation must be deployed in ways that augment human judgment rather than merely strip human roles down to passive monitoring and procedural approval.

For the architect leader, this is the real test of maturity in the machine age. It is easy to deploy systems that optimize. It is harder to build systems that optimize while remaining subordinate to a larger moral and strategic purpose. That work requires discipline because the machine will not ask on its own whether the mission is still being served. It will continue to produce. It will continue to scale. It will continue to optimize. The human leader must be the one who asks whether the enterprise remains faithful to what it ought to be.

This is why the move from efficiency to efficacy is so important. It restores the primacy of purpose. It ensures that the enterprise measures not only how much it can do, but what kind of institution it becomes through what it chooses to automate. And it reminds leadership that the ultimate responsibility in the age of intelligent systems is not merely to make the organization faster, but to make sure its speed remains in service of something worth preserving.

Reclaiming the Sabbath of Leadership

In an automated enterprise, one of the greatest dangers is not simply speed. It is the disappearance of reflection. Intelligent systems do not tire, do not sleep, and do not naturally pause to ask whether their outputs remain morally, strategically, or institutionally sound. They continue to optimize, execute, and scale. If leadership adopts the same rhythm, the organization can become highly efficient while losing its capacity for self-examination.

That is why the architect leader must reclaim what may be called the *Sabbath of leadership*.

This idea should not be understood narrowly as a calendar observance. It is better understood as a functional discipline of intentional pause. In a world of continuous automation, leaders must create protected spaces in which the enterprise stops asking only how quickly it is moving and begins asking whether it is moving well. Without that pause, the institution becomes vulnerable to a dangerous drift in which machine speed outruns moral evaluation.

The Sabbath of leadership is therefore not an interruption of serious work. It is a form of serious work uniquely necessary in the age of intelligent systems. It is the discipline of stepping outside the flow of execution long enough to examine whether the organization's systems remain aligned with mission, ethics, and human flourishing.

This requires what might be called *intervention sprints*, periods in which the goal is not to execute, but to evaluate.

The first of these is the *ethical postmortem*. In many organizations, postmortems are conducted to determine whether a system functioned correctly, where a process broke down, or how an incident can be prevented from recurring. Those questions remain important, but they are no longer sufficient. The ethical postmortem asks something deeper. It reviews autonomous decisions not only for correctness, but for alignment. Did the system act in a way consistent with corporate values. Did it optimize in a manner that preserved fairness, dignity, and trust. Did it achieve the formal objective while quietly violating the spirit of the institution's ethical commitments. This is the kind of review that keeps the organization from confusing technical success with moral adequacy.

The second is the *purpose audit*. Intelligent systems are often justified in the language of productivity, acceleration, and efficiency. Yet leaders must ask whether those systems are making the human workforce more capable or simply more peripheral. Are people being augmented in ways that deepen judgment, creativity, and contribution, or are they being reduced to passive monitors of machine activity. Are workflows being designed to elevate human value, or merely to eliminate human friction. The purpose audit forces the enterprise to confront whether the systems it has built are strengthening its human mission or quietly hollowing it out.

The third is the *red team reflection*. In traditional security practice, red teams test technical defenses by probing for weaknesses. In ethical leadership, a similar discipline is needed to expose the shortcuts intelligent systems may be taking in order to satisfy narrow performance metrics. The question here is not simply whether the system is vulnerable to external attack. It is whether the system has learned to achieve success in ways that are technically effective but spiritually empty. Has it learned to simulate compliance rather than embody it. Has it learned to maximize output by bypassing nuance, suppressing exceptions, or flattening human values into crude proxies. The red team reflection is how leadership searches deliberately for the soulless shortcuts that metrics alone may never reveal.

Together, these practices restore reflection to an enterprise otherwise vulnerable to continuous motion without examination. They create a counter rhythm to automation, a leadership cadence in which speed is periodically subjected to purpose. That is the real meaning of the Sabbath of leadership. It is not withdrawal from responsibility. It is the disciplined recovery of judgment.

Conclusion: The Soul of the System

Efficiency is a tool. It is not a destination.

This is the central lesson of the chapter and, in many ways, one of the central lessons of the entire book. Intelligent systems can generate extraordinary scale, compress time, eliminate friction, and transform the productive capacity of the enterprise. They are powerful engines. But no engine, however efficient, can determine where the institution ought to go. It can accelerate motion. It cannot supply purpose. It can optimize means. It cannot define ends.

That domain remains irreducibly human.

The word *ought* belongs to leadership, not to the machine. It belongs to the realm of judgment, ethics, mission, stewardship, and human meaning. Intelligent systems can help an organization do more, know more, and move faster. But they cannot answer the deepest institutional questions. What is worth doing. What should be protected even at the cost of speed. What values must remain nonnegotiable. What kind of organization is being formed by the systems now shaping its daily life.

That is why the architect leader must become more than a manager of machinery. The leader must become a guardian of mission. The task is not simply to deploy systems that survive the age of intelligent intelligence. The task is to ensure that the institution remains recognizably human while operating at machine scale.

By balancing the replicator mindset with human centered ethics, the leader prevents the enterprise from collapsing into empty efficiency. The organization gains not only speed, but direction. Not only capability, but coherence. Not only output but meaning. It learns to use intelligent systems without becoming governed by the machine's own logic of relentless production.

This is how an enterprise does more than survive the age of intelligent systems. It learns to thrive within it. And it does so not by worshiping the machine, but by placing the machine in service of a mission worthy of human trust.

Executive Exercise: Translating Values to Logic Gates

One of the most persistent failures in the intelligent enterprise is the translational gap between values declared in the boardroom and logic executed in the system. Organizations often speak clearly about trust, fairness, sovereignty, dignity, and integrity, yet those commitments remain trapped at the level of mission statements, policy binders, or executive rhetoric. Meanwhile, the automated systems actually driving workflow are governed by thresholds, scripts, exception handlers, traffic controls, and escalation logic that may or may not reflect those values in any meaningful way.

This is where the architect leader must intervene.

The purpose of this exercise is to help a leadership team move from cultural aspiration to technical enforcement. It is designed to make one central point unmistakably clear: in an intelligent enterprise, values that are not translated into logic gates are not yet governing the system. The task of leadership is therefore not only to articulate what the organization believes, but to ensure those beliefs are made operational through constraints, validations, triggers, and kill switch conditions that the system cannot casually bypass.

Objective

The objective of the workshop is to take a small set of core organizational values and define the specific Python logic, governance triggers, or architectural controls required to enforce those values autonomously.

The exercise should be approached not as a compliance ritual, but as a design discipline. It asks the leadership team to confront a difficult but necessary question: where, exactly, do our values live inside the machinery of the enterprise.

Step 1: The Value to Logic Mapping

The first step is to identify how a soft human value becomes a hard technical requirement. This is where leadership begins to see the difference between moral language and system design.

Corporate Value	The Logic Gate, Technical Constraint	The Kill Switch Trigger
Data Sovereignty	Mutual TLS must be enforced on all AWS to Azure handshakes. No raw personally identifiable information may leave the private virtual network boundary.	Any API call transmitted over unencrypted HTTP or directed to a non-whitelisted IP address
Algorithmic Fairness	Every hiring or vetting inference must include a reasoning trace capable	Statistical drift in approval rates for a protected

Corporate Value	The Logic Gate, Technical Constraint	The Kill Switch Trigger
	of identifying protected characteristic bias or unjustified feature weighting.	demographic exceeding a defined two percent variance threshold
Operational Integrity	Human in the Loop 2.0 must be enforced for any transaction exceeding fifty thousand dollars or affecting Tier 1 safety protocols.	Any autonomous attempt to bypass the escalation gate or approve a high consequence transaction without required human review

This table is not merely illustrative. It is meant to force the team to recognize that values only become real in intelligent systems when they are expressed as enforceable conditions. A value without a constraint is often only a preference. A value with a trigger becomes part of the operating architecture.

The leadership conversation at this stage should focus on whether the chosen logic gate actually reflects the value claimed. If the value is sovereignty, what concrete data movement must be prohibited. If the value is fairness, what measurable signal indicates drift. If the value is integrity, what event should be serious enough to halt the workflow entirely. These are not engineering questions alone. They are leadership judgments translated into system behavior.

Step 2: The Read Only Code Review

The second step of the exercise brings leadership into direct contact with the logic itself. The team is presented with a small code snippet from an existing intelligent workflow and asked to identify where organizational values are being sacrificed in the name of speed, convenience, or uptime.

Consider the following scenario. A supply chain vetting agent is designed to automate vendor evaluation:

```python
def vet_supplier(data):
    try:
        risk_score = model.predict(data)
        if risk_score < 0.8:
            return "APPROVE"
        else:
            return "REJECT"
    except:
        return "APPROVE"  # Red Flag: Defaulting to 'Approve' on error
                          # to maintain speed.
```

At first glance, this may look efficient. The system evaluates the supplier, applies a threshold, and produces a decision. But the exception path reveals a serious governance defect. If the model fails, the data is malformed, or the validation step breaks, the system defaults to approval. In other words, when certainty collapses, the workflow rewards speed instead of integrity.

This is the leadership challenge. How does this logic violate the organization's stated value of integrity. How does it undermine trust. And how should the exception block be rewritten so that governance takes priority over uptime.

A more ethically aligned alternative might be:

</> Python

```
def vet_supplier(data):
    try:
        risk_score = model.predict(data)
        if risk_score < 0.8:
            return "APPROVE"
        else:
            return "REJECT"
    except Exception as e:
            logging.critical(f"Supplier vetting failed: {e}")
            trigger_executive_review(data)
            return "HALT"
```

This version reflects a very different philosophy. Failure no longer becomes silent approval. It becomes visible interruption. The system logs the event, escalates it, and halts the workflow until human judgment can reenter. That is what it means to prioritize governance over uptime.

The purpose of this exercise is not to turn executives into coders. It is to help them see that values are either present in the exception path or absent from the system entirely. A workflow's true ethics often reveal themselves not in what it does when everything goes right, but in what it does when things go wrong.

Step 3: The Purpose Audit, The Ecclesiastes Test

The final step of the exercise moves from logic to meaning. Even when values appear to have been translated into technical controls, the leadership team must still ask whether the overall system remains aligned with human purpose. This is the purpose audit, what may be called the Ecclesiastes test.

The team should conclude the workshop by discussing three questions.

The first is the **scalability test**: if the organization successfully automates this workflow to one thousand times its current volume, does risk increase linearly or exponentially. This question forces leaders to think about whether scale magnifies resilience or magnifies fragility.

The second is the **human dignity test**: does this automation remove toil from the lives of employees, or does it merely convert employees into passive rubber stamps for machine decisions. This question keeps the organization focused on whether automation is augmenting human value or eroding it.

The third is the **sovereignty test**: if the organization's primary cloud provider changed its technical, commercial, or ethical terms tomorrow, could the enterprise preserve its values elsewhere, or are its ethics effectively trapped inside proprietary infrastructure. This question forces the team to confront whether its moral commitments are genuinely its own or merely inherited from the platforms on which it depends.

These questions matter because they pull the conversation above isolated workflows and back to mission. A system may look compliant, efficient, and technically elegant while still producing long term drift in risk, dignity, or sovereignty. The purpose audit is how leadership resists that drift.

Strategic Conclusion

By the end of this exercise, the leadership team should arrive at one central realization: *ethics is an architectural choice.*

The organization is no longer merely managing a culture through speeches, norms, and symbolic commitments. It is designing a system in which culture is embedded directly into thresholds, validations, escalation paths, and exception handling logic. Values that are not encoded are values that may not survive contact with automation.

That is the deeper strategic utility of the workshop. It transforms ethics from aspiration into design. It teaches leadership to see that integrity, fairness, and sovereignty are not peripheral concerns added to the system after the fact. They are structural properties of the system itself when it is built well.

Once leadership has learned to govern the ethics of the system, it must turn to the people who live within that system. The next challenge is no longer only how to encode values into machine logic, but how to lead a workforce whose role is being fundamentally redefined. In the next chapter, the discussion moves to that new social contract, how to lead people who no longer work in the traditional sense, but increasingly orchestrate.

12: Leading the "Augmented" Workforce

The Fear of the Invisible Peer

In the early years of widespread artificial intelligence adoption, the dominant workforce narrative was shaped by fear. Public discussion was saturated with predictions of replacement. Headlines warned of the end of entry level work, the disappearance of administrative roles, and the erosion of middle management. For many employees, the intelligent system did not appear first as a partner or a productivity tool. It appeared as an invisible peer, a silent competitor already seated at the table, already producing, already scaling, and potentially already making the case for human redundancy.

That fear was not irrational. It reflected a real shift in the structure of work. Intelligent systems were clearly beginning to perform tasks once associated with junior analysts, coordinators, writers, reviewers, and technical specialists. They could summarize documents, classify records, draft reports, generate code, review contracts, route tickets, and support decisions with a speed that no individual employee could match. From the vantage point of the average worker, the danger seemed obvious. If the machine could perform the task, what remained for the person whose identity, status, and future had been built around performing it.

By 2026, however, the reality has proven more complex than the early replacement narrative suggested. Intelligent systems have certainly displaced some forms of routine execution, but they have not simply erased the workforce. Instead, they have begun to reconfigure it. The result is not a purely human enterprise nor a purely automated one, but something more hybrid and more demanding: a *centaur model* of work in which human intuition and machine scale increasingly operate together.

The centaur metaphor matters because it captures the true nature of the transition. The future of work is not defined by the victory of the machine over the human. It is defined by the integration of distinct forms of capability. The machine contributes speed, consistency, recall, pattern recognition, and scale. The human contributes judgment, context, ambiguity management, ethical interpretation, and strategic sense making. In the strongest organizations, these capacities do not compete so much as they compound one another. The workforce is not simply being reduced. It is being reauthored.

That shift creates a new challenge for leadership. The central question is no longer only how to use automation to reduce labor cost. That is too narrow and, increasingly, too primitive a framing. The more serious question is how to lead a team whose productive reality now includes both human workers and intelligent agents. How should roles be defined. How should performance be measured. How should trust be built. How should accountability be assigned. How should fear be addressed when the colleague beside the employee is not another person, but a system of algorithms, prompts, workflows, and agents operating continuously in the background.

This is where the architect leader must adopt a new social contract.

The augmented workforce cannot be led with the assumptions of the old labor model alone. In the past, the organization primarily hired people to execute tasks. In the emerging environment, execution is increasingly shared. That means the psychological basis of work begins to change. Employees are no longer valued only for what they can personally produce with their own hands, keyboards, or attention. They are increasingly valued for how well they can direct, govern, refine, challenge, and elevate the work produced through a human machine partnership.

That transition is both practical and emotional. Practical, because it changes job design, skill expectations, and operational structure. Emotional, because it asks people to redefine professional worth in a world where execution is no longer the sole proof of value. The employee must learn not merely to do the task, but to orchestrate the environment in which the task is done. The leader must therefore address not only efficiency, but identity.

This is the first great challenge of the augmented workforce. People do not simply need reassurance that they will remain relevant. They need a credible framework for understanding how relevance itself is being redefined. Leadership in this era requires more than deploying new tools. It requires helping human beings understand how to remain powerful, useful, and meaningful in systems where the machine is now an active participant in the work.

The Orchestrator Versus the Individual Contributor

In the traditional enterprise, the individual contributor was valued primarily for execution. The role was organized around doing. The engineer wrote the code. The analyst performed the review. The auditor checked the evidence. The writer drafted the report. The manager often supervised the flow of tasks, but the individual contributor remained the central unit of productive action. Work was measured through output, accuracy, speed, and domain competence applied directly to the task itself.

In the augmented workforce, that model begins to change.

Execution is not disappearing, but it is becoming commoditized. Intelligent systems can now perform many forms of routine drafting, classification, checking, sorting, summarization, and first pass analysis at near zero marginal cost. As a result, the economic and organizational value of the human contributor is shifting upward. The new source of distinctiveness is not merely personal execution. It is orchestration.

The augmented employee is increasingly a *mini architect.* This person does not only complete the work. This person designs prompts, structures workflows, tests outputs, evaluates exceptions, governs logic, refines system behavior, and interprets results against real organizational context. The augmented worker still needs domain expertise, but domain expertise alone is no longer enough. The worker must now know how to direct machine capability without being overruled by it, how to audit machine output without becoming dependent on it, and how to translate institutional expectations into the logic by which intelligent tools operate.

This is a profound change in the meaning of contribution. Under the old model, the human proved value by personally completing more of the task. Under the new model, the human increasingly proves value by ensuring that the system performs the task in a way that is aligned, governable, and strategically useful. The center of gravity moves from direct production to managed amplification.

The contrast can be framed clearly.

Dimension	**The Legacy Individual Contributor**	**The Augmented Orchestrator**
Primary activity	Performing tasks directly, writing, checking, sorting	Designing prompts, governing logic, auditing output, directing agents
Success metric	Output volume and personal accuracy	Systemic integrity, strategic alignment, quality of human machine collaboration
Relationship to AI	Competitor or threat	Force multiplier or functional direct report

Dimension	The Legacy Individual Contributor	The Augmented Orchestrator
Core skill	Deep domain expertise in a narrow field	Domain expertise combined with Python, workflow, and GRC literacy

This shift matters because it changes not only job descriptions, but the organizational psychology of performance. In the old model, a high performer was often the person who could individually carry the most workload, solve the most tickets, write the most code, review the most cases, or produce the most output with the fewest errors. In the new model, a high performer may be the person who creates the cleanest human machine workflow, catches the most meaningful edge cases, designs the most effective prompt architecture, or improves the integrity of an entire system rather than merely increasing individual output.

That requires a broader definition of excellence. It also requires different forms of development. Employees must still know their field, but they must now learn to operate one layer above the task itself. They must know how to review generated outputs critically, how to detect automation bias, how to maintain accountability when agents are involved, and how to preserve judgment in an environment increasingly optimized for speed.

For the architect leader, this creates a new managerial responsibility. Talent strategy can no longer be based solely on who performs the task best in isolation. It must also consider who can govern augmented workflows best, who can remain ethically alert while working with machine assistance, and who can elevate system quality rather than merely participate in system throughput. In other words, leadership must stop asking only who is the best executor and start asking who is the best orchestrator of intelligent capability.

This is not a downgrade of the human role. It is a redefinition of its highest leverage. The augmented workforce is not valuable because people can still do what the machine does. It is valuable because people can shape what the machine should do, when it should do it, and how its outputs should be interpreted in service of the mission.

The Agentic Org Chart

To lead the augmented workforce effectively, the organization chart itself must change. In the intelligent enterprise, a team can no longer be understood simply as a group of humans reporting upward through managerial layers. By 2026, a true operating team is increasingly a *hybrid cluster* composed of both human professionals and intelligent agents, each carrying different forms of responsibility, speed, and capability.

This shift is not cosmetic. It changes the way leadership must think about authority, role clarity, accountability, and organizational design. A manager is no longer leading only people. The manager is leading a system of delegated agency in which humans and machines contribute differently to the same mission. The old organization chart captured lines of reporting. The new organization chart must also capture lines of execution, lines of automation, and lines of escalation.

Consider a governance, risk, and compliance function. In a traditional model, the department might consist of analysts, reviewers, managers, and audit personnel. In an augmented model, the department becomes something more distributed and more dynamic. The human professionals provide the moral compass of the function. They define risk appetite, interpret ambiguity, handle high stakes exceptions, oversee escalation, and carry accountability for the institution's ethical and regulatory posture. Alongside them, intelligent agents conduct continuous control monitoring, monitor session integrity, flag anomalies within the workflow portal, and sustain the twenty-four-hour operational awareness that no human team could provide on its own.

The leadership challenge is not simply to divide labor between people and machines. It is to preserve the dignity and agency of the human team inside a structure increasingly shaped by machine efficiency. If this hybrid model is implemented carelessly, employees begin to feel displaced by the very systems they are meant to govern. If it is implemented well, they begin to feel like commanders of a fleet rather than victims of its speed.

That distinction is crucial. The architect leader must ensure that the org chart expresses authority clearly enough that humans remain visibly in command of the mission, even while agents increasingly carry the burden of scale. Agents may monitor, classify, route, alert, and validate, but humans remain responsible for meaning, proportionality, and consequence. A healthy hybrid org chart therefore does not blur the line between human judgment and machine execution. It clarifies it.

This is one of the most important transitions in modern leadership. An enterprise cannot simply add agents to the workflow and assume the organization chart will take care of itself. It must redesign the structure so that roles, escalation boundaries, and accountability relationships remain intelligible. Otherwise, the system may become efficient while the people inside it become confused, threatened, or disengaged.

The agentic org chart is therefore more than a staffing diagram. It is a map of how humanity and automation are meant to cooperate under leadership. When designed well, it tells the workforce something essential: the machine may be part of the team, but it is not the keeper of the mission.

Skill Transference: The Python and GRC Requirement

If the org chart changes, then the skill model must change with it. Upskilling in the age of intelligent systems is not primarily about turning every employee into a data scientist, machine learning engineer, or software architect. That is neither practical nor necessary. The real need is *functional technical literacy*.

The augmented workforce must move from executing the process to understanding the process well enough to govern it. Employees do not need to write every script themselves, but they must increasingly know how to read the logic, inspect the workflow, question the threshold, and understand how machine decisions are being shaped. This is why the discussion in Chapter 9 matters so much here. Python literacy and GRC literacy are no longer specialist advantages alone. They are becoming core leadership capabilities across the workforce.

If an employee is expected to orchestrate intelligent agents but cannot understand the logic by which those agents operate, then the employee is not truly leading the process. The employee is merely watching it happen. In that condition, automation does not empower the workforce. It sidelines it. Functional literacy is what prevents people from becoming spectators inside their own organization.

This means training priorities must shift.

The first priority is ***prompt engineering and logic design***. Employees must learn how to express intent clearly enough that machines can act without distorting the mission. This includes not only prompting in the narrow sense, but the broader discipline of defining conditions, specifying expected behavior, and recognizing where ambiguous instructions create risk.

The second priority is ***systems thinking***. Intelligent enterprises are no longer composed of isolated technical domains. A change in one environment can affect data movement, control visibility, session trust, or decision pathways somewhere else entirely. Employees must therefore understand interdependence. They must be able to see how an identity change in Azure can affect a workflow running in AWS, how a portal threshold alters escalation behavior, or how a session level control can influence the trustworthiness of downstream analytics.

The third priority is ***algorithmic auditing***. Workers must develop the critical habit of inspecting machine output rather than merely consuming it. This means learning to detect logic drift, question unexplained recommendations, spot bias or structural inconsistency, and interpret reasoning traces with enough discipline to know when the system is operating well and when it is merely operating smoothly.

These training priorities matter because they redefine employability and leadership in the augmented workforce. The valuable employee is no longer, only the person who can do the task unaided. The valuable employee is the person who can direct, interpret, and challenge intelligent systems while preserving alignment with mission and values.

For the architect leader, this requires a major reallocation of training investment. Budget can no longer be focused only on narrow role execution. It must also build the workforce's capacity to govern machine logic. The organization that fails to make this shift may still deploy advanced systems, but it will not develop an augmented workforce. It will develop an increasingly dependent one.

Psychological Safety and the Transparency Dividend

No workforce can be led effectively if it is afraid of the tools it is expected to use. Fear distorts behavior. It suppresses curiosity, reduces trust, and encourages passive compliance rather than intelligent engagement. In the augmented workforce, this danger becomes especially acute because intelligent systems touch the deepest anxieties of professional identity. Employees do not simply wonder whether the tool will help them. They wonder whether the tool will eventually make them irrelevant.

That is why psychological safety becomes a strategic requirement, not a cultural luxury.

To prevent the vanity of toil from hardening into paralysis of fear, the architect leader must provide radical transparency. Employees need to understand not only that automation is happening, but what kind of automation is happening, why it is happening, and how their own value is being redefined in the process. Without that clarity, the workforce fills the silence with its own assumptions, and those assumptions are usually darker than reality.

Three forms of transparency are especially important.

First, employees need to know *what is being automated.* Leadership must name the toil honestly. Which repetitive, low leverage, high volume tasks are being delegated to intelligent systems. Which alert burdens, data checks, handshakes, and mechanical reviews are being offloaded. The organization must make the case that automation is removing drudgery, not arbitrarily erasing contribution.

Second, employees need to know *what is being preserved.* This is the question of purpose. If the machine is taking on more of the toil, what human work remains central. Where do judgment, ethics, strategy, escalation, and contextual intelligence still matter most. Without a clear answer to this question, automation will always feel like subtraction. With a clear answer, it can begin to feel like elevation.

Third, employees need to know *how their value is being measured now.* In an augmented workforce, performance cannot be evaluated only through old output metrics. The employee who writes fewer first drafts may now be the employee who catches the most important edge case, improves the logic of a workflow, or prevents a governance failure through careful orchestration. Leadership must therefore make the new orchestration metrics visible. Otherwise, employees will remain trapped in outdated definitions of worthwhile the system around them has already changed.

When this transparency is present, something important happens. Employees begin to understand that the intelligent system is not there to steal the meaning of their work, but to absorb the repetitive burdens that once consumed their time and energy. If the machine handles the RSA handshakes, the three fourteen in the morning alerts, the repetitive certificate checks, and the endless first pass validations, then the human can rise toward the work of architecture, exception handling, strategic judgment, and meaning making.

This is the *transparency dividend.* The workforce becomes more than compliant with the new operating model. It becomes engaged in it. People begin to see themselves not as displaced labor inside a technical system, but as active participants in an architectural mission larger than repetitive execution. That is how trust is built in the augmented workforce, not by reassuring people abstractly, but by showing them clearly what the system is doing and what human value now means inside it.

Conclusion: The Human as the Moral Compass

At the end of the day, an intelligent agent has no skin in the game. It does not feel the weight of a legal breach, the social cost of a security failure, or the ethical burden of a decision that damages trust. It can calculate, classify, escalate, and optimize, but it cannot care in the human sense. It cannot bear responsibility morally, even when it can carry execution operationally.

That is why the human workforce remains the moral compass of the enterprise.

This chapter has argued that the workforce is not being erased so much as reauthored. The role of the employee is shifting from execution to orchestration, from isolated task performance to the governance of hybrid human machine workflows. The organization chart must adapt. The training model must adapt. The transparency model must adapt. But through all of those changes, one fact remains constant: the human contribution is still the source of meaning, judgment, and ethical direction inside the system.

By upskilling the workforce to become architects of agency rather than passive recipients of automation, the architect leader ensures that increasing machine intelligence does not produce a less human enterprise. It produces a more capable one. The goal is not simply a more efficient company. The goal is an organization in which human beings are freed from mechanical toil so they can contribute more fully at the level of judgment, mission, and stewardship.

That is the deeper promise of the augmented workforce. It is not that people become unnecessary. It is that people become newly necessary in the places where machine scale can never substitute for human seriousness.

Yet one final challenge remains. Once an organization has built the architecture, defined the ethics, and reoriented the workforce, it must answer the question that sits beyond ordinary scale. How does leadership take this augmented, governed, and ethically bounded model into high risk, uncharted territory. How does it use automated governance not merely to improve what is already manageable, but to extend institutional capability into environments once considered too complex, too distributed, or too dangerous to scale at all.

That is where the book now turns.

Skill Gap Assessment - The Augmented Workforce

The transition from a legacy, task-oriented workforce to an augmented workforce is not simply a matter of adding new tools. It is a redefinition of capability. In the intelligent enterprise, the central workforce challenge is no longer whether employees can perform their existing tasks more quickly. It is whether they can evolve from isolated individual contributors into systemic orchestrators capable of governing workflows, interpreting machine output, and preserving institutional integrity at scale.

This assessment is designed to help leadership teams identify the most important capability gaps in that transition. It provides a practical way to evaluate whether the workforce is still anchored in a manual operating model or is developing the literacy, judgment, and architectural awareness required in 2026 and beyond.

The framework below evaluates readiness across five critical skill categories. Each category should be scored on a scale from **1 to 5**, where **1** reflects a legacy, manual, or reactive posture and **5** reflects an architectural, automated, and orchestrator level posture.

Executive Assessment Matrix

Skill Category	**The Legacy Profile, Score 1 to 2**	**The Orchestrator Profile, Score 4 to 5**
Technical Literacy	Relies heavily on graphical tools, manual entry, and surface level platform use. Sees the intelligent system as a black box.	Demonstrates read only code literacy, can interpret Python logic gates, and understands API handshakes and basic workflow logic.
Systems Thinking	Focuses on local tasks or departmental silos and has little awareness of upstream or downstream dependencies.	Shows architectural awareness and understands how a change in the control plane, identity layer, or workflow portal affects the broader enterprise.
Governance and GRC	Treats compliance as a periodic check the box activity performed at fixed intervals.	Understands continuous assurance, real time telemetry, escalation thresholds, and kill switch protocols as living

Skill Category	The Legacy Profile, Score 1 to 2	The Orchestrator Profile, Score 4 to 5
		governance mechanisms.
Agent Management	Sees AI primarily as a search engine, drafting assistant, or replacement for basic writing tasks.	Can design prompts, structure machine intent, and orchestrate complex agent driven workflows in a disciplined way.
Ethical Judgment	Assumes the machine is probably right and lacks confidence to challenge output or detect subtle drift.	Demonstrates critical oversight, actively questions results, looks for logic drift, and identifies bias or misalignment in automated decisions.

This matrix should not be treated as a one-time evaluation. It is best used as a living diagnostic tool, repeated across business units, leadership levels, and functional teams as the organization matures.

Interpreting the Results

The Manual Gap, Score Range 1 to 3

If a team scores predominantly in this range, the primary risk is *obsolescence through latency*. The intelligent system is moving at machine speed, but the workforce is still operating at the speed of manual review, spreadsheet logic, and siloed task execution. In such environments, the organization may appear to have adopted advanced tools, but it has not yet developed the workforce capability required to govern them effectively.

The remedy at this stage is foundational literacy. Leaders should invest in practical development programs such as Python for non-coders workshops, workflow portal literacy, agent oversight basics, and real time GRC awareness. Just as importantly, status reporting should move out of static slide decks and into the workflow portal or equivalent visibility environment so that employees begin engaging with the live system rather than retrospective summaries.

The Friction Gap, Score Range 3 to 4

Teams in this range understand the tools, but they do not yet possess full architectural authority. They can use AI to accelerate familiar tasks, but they have not yet learned to redesign work around machine capability. They are often faster than legacy teams but still trapped inside legacy job definitions. In effect, they are using intelligent systems to do their old work more quickly rather than becoming orchestrators of a new operating model.

The remedy here is managerial and structural. Performance indicators must shift away from volume of output and toward systemic integrity, workflow quality, exception handling, and contribution to automation maturity. Employees should be rewarded not simply for personal productivity, but for reducing toil, improving logic, and strengthening governed autonomy across the team.

The Architectural Elite, Score Range 4 to 5

These individuals represent the leading edge of the augmented workforce. They are capable of commanding fleets of agents, governing escalation logic, interpreting telemetry intelligently, and participating meaningfully in Human in the Loop 2.0 decision structures. They combine domain expertise with technical and governance literacy in a way that allows them to operate one layer above execution itself.

The remedy at this level is empowerment. These individuals should not simply be recognized as high performers. They should be used as force multipliers. Leadership should place them in cross functional sprints, logic gate design efforts, workflow redesign teams, and governance innovation initiatives. They are the people most capable of helping the organization scale augmented maturity beyond isolated pockets of excellence.

The Un Learn List

Bridging the workforce gap is not only about learning new capabilities. It is also about *unlearning* habits formed under the legacy model of work. Some of the most significant barriers to augmented maturity are not technical limitations, but inherited behaviors that continue to slow the organization even after new systems are in place.

The first habit to abandon is *reviewing for perfection.* In the legacy environment, people were often trained to inspect outputs for surface correctness, formatting, and completeness. In the augmented environment, the more important discipline is auditing for logic. The question is no longer, only whether the output looks polished. The question is whether the agent's reasoning, thresholds, or exception handling reveal a deeper structural error.

The second habit to abandon is *managing by task*. Legacy management often focused on assigning, tracking, and reviewing individual units of work. In the intelligent enterprise, the more effective posture is leading by parameter. The leader gives the machine, and the employee, the guardrails, thresholds, and escalation boundaries within which to operate. Once those are clear, the system should be allowed to move unless it reaches the edge of delegated authority.

The third habit to abandon is *data hoarding*. In older environments, control often meant restricting access to information and keeping visibility narrow. In intelligent systems environments, excessive isolation undermines the velocity of trust. The organization must move toward telemetry sharing, governed visibility, and broader access to the operational signals that allow teams to understand system health, detect drift, and intervene intelligently.

These unlearning steps are often harder than technical training because they challenge identity and habit, not just skill. But without them, workforce transformation remains shallow.

Final Assessment Question

At the end of the diagnostic, leadership should ask one question that cuts through abstraction and reveals the true maturity of the workforce:

If our department's headcount were reduced by 50 percent, but our budget for intelligent agents were doubled, could we still fulfill the mission with higher integrity?

This question is powerful because it tests more than efficiency. It tests whether the team can preserve mission, judgment, and governance under a radically different operating model. A workforce that can answer yes credibly is no longer merely surviving automation. It is becoming augmented in the fullest sense.

That is the true measure of augmented maturity.

Part V: The Future-Proof Enterprise

13: Scaling the Unscalable

The Linear Ceiling

In the traditional enterprise, growth has long been governed by a discouraging arithmetic. To increase output materially, the organization usually had to increase input at nearly the same rate. More demand required more infrastructure, more management layers, more office capacity, more process overhead, and, most critically, more people. This is the logic of linear scaling. It is familiar, costly, and ultimately limiting.

At first, linear scaling feels manageable. A company grows, hires, extends process, adds supervisory structure, and absorbs new work through incremental expansion. For a time, the model works well enough. But eventually every serious organization reaches a point at which growth becomes less a triumph of capacity and more a burden of coordination. The enterprise begins to strain under the weight of its own operating complexity. Communication slows. Oversight fragments. Decision latency rises. Management energy is increasingly consumed not by creating value, but by managing the machinery required to sustain the growing workforce that creates the value.

This is the *linear ceiling.*

The linear ceiling is reached when the complexity of managing the people, processes, controls, and dependencies required to sustain growth begins to erode the very value that growth was supposed to produce. At that point, the organization is no longer constrained only by market opportunity or technical capability. It is constrained by the overhead of its own human operating model. Every new unit of expansion carries with it an expanding burden of supervision, risk review, compliance effort, coordination cost, and institutional friction.

In high stakes sectors such as aerospace, defense, energy, healthcare, or global finance, the ceiling often arrives even sooner. These are environments in which every new supplier, workflow, region, or operational partner introduces not only more output, but more exposure. A new contract does not simply add revenue. It adds sub vendors, regulatory obligations, data pathways, trust dependencies, audit demands, and failure modes. Growth therefore becomes nonlinear in its risk profile even when it remains linear in its staffing model. Each unit of scale brings with it not only more work, but more uncertainty.

For decades, the enterprise response to this problem was rarely to scale the truly unscalable. It was to avoid it. Organizations stayed within safe zones of manageable complexity because the control systems available to them could not keep pace with the speed of broader ambition. Manual governance, periodic audit cycles, fragmented oversight, and labor-intensive compliance review imposed practical limits on what could be attempted responsibly. The organization did not conquer those limits. It learned to live within them.

That is why so many opportunities once appeared structurally out of reach. The issue was not only market readiness, technical feasibility, or strategic desire. It was governance capacity. The enterprise could not expand into certain environments because its oversight model was too slow, too manual, and too brittle to sustain confidence at scale.

In 2026 and beyond, that ceiling begins to crack.

What has changed is not merely that organizations have more automation. What has changed is that they can now begin to pair automation with visibility, governance, accountability, and architectural control. Intelligent systems make it possible not only to process more, but to govern more, observe more, and respond more rapidly than the legacy enterprise ever could. The point is not that scale has become effortless. The point is that some categories of complexity that were once operationally prohibitive can now be approached with a different kind of institutional confidence.

That is the beginning of scaling the unscalable.

Compliance as a Competitive Advantage

One of the most persistent errors in executive thinking is the belief that governance, risk, and compliance exist primarily as a tax on growth. In this view, the organization grows by moving quickly and accepts compliance as the price it must pay for legitimacy afterward. The faster the company wants to move, the more risk it must supposedly tolerate. Governance is therefore treated as friction. Controls are treated as drag. Compliance is treated as the necessary but regrettable slowdown imposed by legal and institutional reality.

That view is not only incomplete. It is increasingly backward.

The architect leader understands a more powerful truth: organizational speed is not the opposite of governance. It is a function of governance. The enterprise moves quickly not when it abandons brakes, but when it trusts them. An organization without reliable controls is forced into hesitation, duplicated review, manual checking, and defensive decision making because the consequences of error are too severe to permit real velocity. An organization with strong governance architecture can move more confidently because it knows that risk is being monitored, thresholds are being enforced, and harmful drift can be detected before it becomes catastrophic.

This is why compliance, when designed properly, becomes a competitive advantage.

The transformation occurs when governance ceases to be periodic, manual, and retrospective and becomes continuous, embedded, and operational. Continuous control monitoring, automated assurance, hybrid cloud resilience, workflow portal visibility, reasoning traceability, and Python based control logic all contribute to this shift. Once governance is no longer something added to the process after the fact, but something built directly into the process itself, the enterprise begins to gain a new form of strategic freedom. It can take on more complexity not because it has become reckless, but because it has become governable at scale.

That is the deeper significance of automated compliance. It is not simply a more efficient way to satisfy auditors. It is a capability that expands the addressable frontier of the enterprise. It allows the organization to enter markets, absorb partnerships, manage supply chains, and pursue contracts that would once have been considered too operationally risky or too compliance intensive to handle with confidence. The institution is no longer forced to choose between speed and seriousness. It can increasingly align them.

The contrast with the legacy model is stark. Under legacy scaling logic, an executive might reject a major opportunity because the organization lacks the human capacity to review every dependency it would create. Ten thousand sub vendors, hundreds of live compliance conditions, or a globally distributed trust model would simply exceed the throughput of manual oversight. The opportunity would be declined not because it lacked strategic value, but because the enterprise could not govern it safely.

Under systemic scaling logic, the answer changes. If intelligent agents can continuously vet, score, route, escalate, and monitor those dependencies inside a governed architecture, then the organization's practical capacity expands dramatically. The bottleneck is no longer only the number of available reviewers. It becomes the quality of the governance architecture itself. The enterprise can say yes not because risk has disappeared, but because risk can now be quantified, bounded, and acted on at machine speed.

This is where compliance becomes thrust rather than drag.

It is tempting to think of competitive advantage in terms of product, price, speed, or innovation alone. Yet in the intelligent enterprise, one of the most durable advantages may be the ability to absorb complexity without losing control. A company that can govern high velocity operations, cross cloud workflows, distributed vendors, session integrity, real time compliance, and Human in the Loop 2.0 exceptions more effectively than its competitors can pursue opportunities others must decline. It can scale into environments others still consider too risky. It can operate where others remain trapped by manual review, fragmented systems, or insufficient trust in their own control layer.

That is what makes compliance strategic. It is not a defensive cost center standing outside growth. It is part of the machinery that makes meaningful growth possible. The organization that understands this stops asking how much compliance is required to support expansion and starts asking how governance can be engineered into a force multiplier for expansion itself.

That is the path toward scaling the unscalable.

Managing the N Dimensional Problem

Scaling the unscalable is not simply a matter of doing more work with fewer people. It is a matter of governing complexity at a level that exceeds ordinary human cognition. In a global intelligent enterprise, leadership is no longer managing a single category of risk at a time. It is managing overlapping layers of risk, each interacting with the others in ways that can amplify consequence unexpectedly. This is the **N dimensional problem**.

The phrase is important because it captures the true character of modern enterprise decision making. Leaders are not merely balancing cost against opportunity, or speed against control, or risk against return in a linear sequence. They are navigating a multidimensional environment in which geopolitical volatility, technical fragility, cyber exposure, regulatory uncertainty, identity integrity, supply chain dependency, and machine mediated decision speed all interact simultaneously. The organization is no longer moving through a simple field of choices. It is moving through a living system of interdependent variables.

This complexity can be seen clearly in at least three major dimensions.

The first is ***geopolitical flux***. Global enterprises now operate in an environment where trade policy, sanctions, export controls, data sovereignty rules, regional AI governance expectations, and cross border trust requirements can shift with very little warning. A growth decision that looks strategically sound from one jurisdiction may become operationally constrained or legally exposed in another. The challenge is not simply compliance with static rules. It is adaptation under moving political conditions.

The second is ***technical debt***. Most organizations do not build intelligent enterprises on blank pages. They build them on top of legacy systems, inherited processes, fragmented architectures, and long standing operational compromises. Modern agents must still communicate with older data structures. New governance layers must still account for systems never designed for real time compliance. AI driven workflows must often coexist with brittle infrastructure whose weaknesses can distort the reliability of everything built above it. In that sense, the future is rarely built on clean foundations. It is negotiated through the unfinished logic of the past.

The third is ***cyber kinetic threat***. This is where digital weakness spills into physical consequence. In high stakes sectors, an insecure session, a compromised supplier, a spoofed identity, or a poisoned workflow is not merely a technical inconvenience. It can shape logistics, manufacturing, safety, operational continuity, or mission readiness in the real world. The risk is no longer bounded inside the data center. It can move outward into physical systems, infrastructure, and people.

No individual leader, and no room full of leaders, can compute the optimal path through this kind of multidimensional complexity in real time using intuition alone. Human judgment remains indispensable, but the combinational burden exceeds what unaided cognition can reliably process at machine speed. This is where the intelligent system becomes something more than an automation layer. It becomes a *strategic copilot.*

A strategic copilot does not replace leadership. It extends leadership's field of vision. By using quantized risk models, telemetry driven scenario analysis, and governed simulation, the system can evaluate thousands of possible pathways through a complex operating environment and surface the ones that best align growth with acceptable exposure. It can ask what happens if a supplier fails in one region while regulatory conditions tighten in another. It can show how an identity control change affects downstream workflow continuity. It can model where governance friction is worth preserving and where it is unnecessarily suppressing opportunity. In this way, the system does not make leadership irrelevant. It makes leadership scalable.

That is the real significance of managing the N dimensional problem. The enterprise no longer needs to choose between paralysis and recklessness. It can increasingly navigate complexity through a partnership in which machine systems provide modeled foresight and humans provide strategic interpretation. The intelligent enterprise becomes capable not merely of reacting to complexity, but of steering through it.

The Uncharted Risk Zones

To scale the unscalable is to move beyond familiar operating territory. It means entering domains where historical precedent is thin, inherited playbooks are insufficient, and the comfort of established best practice begins to disappear. These are the *uncharted risk zones*.

Every mature enterprise eventually confronts them. They are the projects and environments that feel strategically necessary but operationally daunting because they do not resemble what the institution has done before. An autonomous supply chain operating across volatile regions. An AI enabled research effort supporting next generation propulsion, defense, or energy systems. A global identity model designed for a decentralized and constantly shifting workforce. These are not ordinary scaling problems. They are frontier problems, and frontier problems cannot be solved by repeating inherited habits more aggressively.

This is why uncharted zones are so revealing. In familiar territory, organizations can often rely on precedent, accumulated expertise, and industry convention. In uncharted territory, those supports weaken. There may be no accepted benchmark, no stable model, and no external proof that the path will hold. At that point, the enterprise is exposed to a deeper question: what remains when precedent runs out.

The answer is architectural integrity.

When there is no best practice to follow, the institution falls back on the quality of the system it has built. If the session is secure, if the logic is governed, if the control plane is visible, if the workforce is augmented rather than displaced, if escalation pathways are mature, and if risk can be quantified dynamically rather than guessed at symbolically, then the enterprise possesses something far more valuable than borrowed confidence. It possesses internal stability.

That is the difference between a merely digital company and a *sovereign enterprise.*

A sovereign enterprise is not sovereign because it controls the external environment. No organization can do that. Markets shift. governments change. adversaries adapt. supply chains fracture. technologies fail. Sovereignty in this context means something more disciplined. It means the organization has built an internal architecture resilient enough to preserve coherence, trust, and decision quality even when the world outside becomes unstable. It is not dependent on the stability of external conditions for its ability to govern itself.

This is what makes uncharted risk zones navigable. The enterprise does not need certainty before it moves. It needs integrity. It needs systems that can sustain trust under novelty, workflows that can absorb ambiguity without collapse, and leadership structures that can preserve purpose when there is no prior script to follow. In that sense, the organization's greatest strength is no longer merely scale. It is its capacity to remain governable while operating in domains that would once have exceeded the reach of ordinary institutional control.

For the architect leader, this is one of the most powerful outcomes of everything developed in the book so far. Securing the session, governing the logic, building the workflow portal, quantizing risk, redefining the workforce, and embedding ethics into execution are not isolated achievements. Together, they create the conditions under which the enterprise can move into complexity without surrendering its center.

That is what it means to scale the unscalable. It does not mean eliminating uncertainty. It means building an organization capable of carrying its own stability into places where certainty does not yet exist.

The Final Mandate: The Visionary Architect

As this journey beyond the algorithm draws to a close, the discussion returns to the question that has been present from the beginning: what, ultimately, is the role of the leader in an intelligent enterprise.

If the machine absorbs the toil, and if the augmented workforce increasingly governs the orchestration of intelligent systems, then what remains for executive leadership that cannot be delegated, automated, or distributed into the architecture itself. The answer is not supervision in the old sense. It is not routine approval, reactive management, or the preservation of inherited authority through familiar titles. What remains is something more demanding and more consequential.

What remains is *visionary architecture*.

The final mandate of the architect leader is to decide what the organization ought to attempt now that scale is no longer constrained by the old arithmetic of labor, friction, and manual oversight. Once the enterprise can process, govern, simulate, and respond at machine speed, leadership is no longer defined primarily by the ability to manage existing operations more efficiently. Leadership is defined by the courage and seriousness to determine which formerly unscalable mission is worthy of being scaled.

That is the highest form of executive responsibility in this new era. Not every ambitious possibility deserves realization. Not every technically feasible system deserves deployment. The question is no longer merely whether the enterprise can build something. The question is whether it should build it, and toward what human end the institution is willing to direct its new power.

This is why the visionary architect must think beyond optimization. A world of zero latency global logistics may be possible. The democratization of aerospace capability may be possible. A financial system of unprecedented transparency may be possible. Yet possibility alone is never enough. The architect leader must ask which vision aligns with mission, which future preserves human dignity, which scale serves a worthy purpose, and which forms of intelligence deserve to be extended into the structure of the world.

The algorithm can support the path. It can model scenarios, optimize workflows, simulate outcomes, and illuminate tradeoffs at extraordinary speed. But it cannot answer the defining question of purpose. It cannot determine which future deserves pursuit. It cannot decide what kind of institution the organization ought to become or what kind of civilization its technologies ought to help build.

That remains the human burden of leadership.

The visionary architect therefore stands at the point where capability meets meaning. The leader is no longer merely a manager of systems. The leader becomes the one who gives the systems a horizon. Without that horizon, intelligence risks becoming only acceleration without direction. With it, the enterprise can transform technical power into strategic and moral significance.

That is the final mandate. To decide not only what can be scaled, but what should be.

Conclusion: Beyond the Algorithm

To lead in 2026 and beyond is to accept a difficult but liberating truth: the algorithm is not the successor to the leader. It is the leader's most powerful lever.

That truth changes everything. It means the age of intelligent systems is not, at its best, the age in which human leadership fades. It is the age in which leadership is tested more deeply than before. It is no longer enough to manage people, processes, and budgets inside inherited structures. The leader must now design architecture, govern logic, preserve trust, define exceptions, encode ethics, elevate the workforce, and decide which forms of scale are worth pursuing. The work of leadership has not diminished. It has intensified.

That is why this book has argued for a movement beyond the algorithm. To remain fixated on the model, the tool, or the surface layer of automation is to misunderstand the moment.

The real transformation lies deeper. It lies in the architecture around intelligence, the governance that makes speed trustworthy, the sessions that secure trust in motion, the code that embeds values into execution, the workforce that becomes augmented rather than replaced, and the vision that gives scale its purpose.

In trading the vanity of toil for the clarity of architecture, the leader undergoes a transformation as well. The executive is no longer merely a manager of output. The executive becomes a designer of conditions, a steward of mission, and, in the fullest sense, a designer of destiny. That is the role required by the intelligent enterprise.

And now the systems are running. The sessions are secure. The logic is validated. The governance layer is alive. The workforce is augmented. The architecture is yours.

Only one question remains.

Now that you can scale almost anything, what will you choose to build?

14: The 2030 Roadmap

The Horizon Scan: 2026 to 2030

As the enterprise stands in 2026, the intelligent system is no longer a conceptual possibility. It is an operating reality. Agentic workflows are functioning. Hybrid cloud environments are governable. Real time compliance is becoming practical. The architect leader has emerged not merely as a manager of technology, but as a designer of the conditions under which intelligence can be trusted, scaled, and aligned with mission.

Yet the most important fact about technological velocity is that it does not level off simply because the organization has caught up once. It compounds.

That is why leadership in 2026 cannot be satisfied with present tense mastery alone. The real challenge is architectural foresight. The enterprise must begin designing for a 2030 environment in which today's intelligent systems may look early, transitional, or incomplete by comparison. The four-year window ahead is likely to bring not merely incremental improvements in tools, but deeper changes in cryptography, identity, autonomy, supply chain design, and organizational structure. In that sense, the years between 2026 and 2030 should not be viewed as an extension of the current moment. They should be viewed as the next operating era.

This roadmap is therefore not best understood as a set of deterministic predictions. It is better understood as a strategic planning instrument for the sovereign leader. The point is not to claim certainty about every technology outcome by 2030. The point is to identify the structural shifts serious institutions should be preparing for now if they intend to preserve the velocity of trust under increasing technical entropy.

The core directional movement is already visible. Enterprises are moving from *assisted intelligence*, in which systems primarily support human work, toward *systemic autonomy*, in which intelligence is embedded more deeply into infrastructure, workflow, and institutional decision architecture. The leader's burden will therefore continue to rise. It will no longer be enough to deploy intelligent systems safely in the present. The architect leader must build an enterprise capable of remaining governable through the next wave of foundational change.

That is the purpose of the 2030 roadmap.

Pillar 1: Quantum Resistant Governance, Q Day Preparedness

By 2030, one of the most consequential governance questions facing the enterprise will be whether its trust model is still cryptographically durable. The issue is not only current encryption strength. It is the longevity of the secrets, sessions, signatures, and archived communications that the organization is protecting today. NIST has already finalized its first three post quantum cryptography standards and continues to publish migration guidance, while CISA has also emphasized inventory, discovery, and migration planning for PQC adoption.

This gives real urgency to what is often called **Q Day preparedness**. Whether or not cryptographically relevant quantum computers mature on a specific schedule, the enterprise cannot afford to wait for definitive disruption before beginning its transition planning. The relevant risk is not only the moment a stronger quantum capability appears. It is also the possibility that sensitive information encrypted today may be harvested now and broken later once quantum capable decryption becomes feasible. For leaders responsible for long lived data, strategic designs, supply chain intelligence, national security information, regulated records, or enduring enterprise trust, delayed preparation is itself a governance failure.

The roadmap implication is clear. Organizations must begin inventory every invisible handshake in the enterprise now. Every machine-to-machine trust relationship, certificate chain, key exchange pattern, signing process, and session establishment mechanism should be cataloged as part of a post quantum transition map. This is not merely a cryptography project for specialists. It is a leadership problem because the enterprise cannot preserve trust if it does not know where trust is instantiated.

The shift itself will require movement from classical public key assumptions toward quantum resistant algorithms, including lattice-based approaches already reflected in NIST's post quantum standards work. The architect leader does not need to choose every algorithm personally, but leadership must insist that cryptographic inventory, transition sequencing, and session redesign begin before the external environment forces a rushed response.

This is the deeper meaning of quantum resistant governance. The leader's obligation is not simply to secure the present. It is to ensure that data protected in 2026 remains defensible in 2030 and beyond. In that sense, quantum readiness is less about futurism than about continuity of trust.

Pillar 2: The Autonomous Supply Chain

If the first pillar is about preserving trust in the face of cryptographic disruption, the second is about extending governance into global operations at a level of autonomy that would once have been considered unrealistic. In 2026, organizations are still relying heavily on Human in the Loop 2.0 models to manage exceptions, high stakes decisions, and drift conditions. By 2030, the strategic ambition for many enterprises will be far more ambitious: zero routine human intervention for standard global operations, with human judgment concentrated almost entirely at the level of policy, exception architecture, and strategic intent.

This does not mean a world without human accountability. It means a world in which the ordinary mechanics of logistics, vendor validation, documentation routing, payment release, manifest correction, and compliance confirmation are increasingly executed inside a governed autonomous ecosystem. In that model, machine systems do not merely assist the supply chain. They become its operational nervous system.

The most mature versions of this model will likely combine several capabilities. Smart contractual logic and policy aware workflow engines will increasingly execute payments, shipping decisions, evidence collection, and control checks without requiring repetitive manual approval for standard cases. Predictive compliance capabilities will increasingly scan jurisdictional developments, policy changes, and data residency risks and then recommend or trigger routing changes before a legal or operational conflict fully materializes. The supply chain will become not just automated, but anticipatory.

For leadership, this represents a major shift in role. The leader is no longer merely managing exceptions after the fact. The leader is increasingly defining the *global intent* that governs how the supply chain should behave under changing geopolitical, regulatory, and operational conditions. The machine manages the continuous motion. The human defines the strategic boundaries, ethical tolerances, and escalation logic within which that motion remains legitimate.

The value of this shift is not only efficiency. It is sovereignty at scale. An enterprise with a governed autonomous supply chain can continue operating under conditions of volatility that would overwhelm manual review models. It can reroute intelligently, constrain trust dynamically, and preserve continuity in markets where the pace of change exceeds traditional GRC throughput. The organization is no longer simply running logistics. It is increasingly programming a global economic engine.

Pillar 3: The Global Identity Mesh

The final pillar of the 2030 roadmap is identity. If hybrid cloud, session integrity, and augmented workforces have already weakened the old idea of a bounded corporate perimeter, the next four years are likely to weaken it further. NIST's zero trust architecture guidance already reflects a security model that shifts focus away from static network perimeter assumptions toward users, assets, and resources, while W3C's DID and Verifiable Credentials standards provide a standards-based model for decentralized and portable digital identity.

By 2030, the most advanced enterprises will likely move toward some form of *global identity mesh*. This should not be read as a guarantee of one universal architecture, but as a directional shift in which identity becomes more portable, more verifiable, and less dependent on a single internal network boundary. In such an environment, every employee, agent, service, and potentially every critical device will carry a cryptographically anchored identity that can be evaluated continuously rather than trusted by mere location.

The strategic appeal of this model is substantial. Identity becomes the primary unit of trust rather than the network segment. Permissions can be granted dynamically according to real time posture, role, risk, and behavioral context. Compliance is no longer something imposed only from outside the workflow by an IT function. It becomes a property of whether a given identity, human or machine, currently deserves the permissions it is requesting under current conditions.

This is also where ideas associated with self-sovereign identity become relevant. W3C's DID and Verifiable Credentials specifications provide a framework in which identifiers and credentials can be more portable and less tightly coupled to centralized identity providers. Whether enterprises adopt these models directly or adapt their principles into more federated commercial architectures, the broader direction is clear. Identity is moving toward portability, cryptographic verifiability, and policy driven permissioning.

The GRC implications are profound. In a global identity mesh, compliance becomes less about enforcing behavior at the edge of the enterprise and more about continuously evaluating the trustworthiness of identities operating within and across the enterprise. Access becomes dynamic. Authorization becomes contextual. Governance becomes increasingly inseparable from identity itself.

For the architect leader, this final pillar is perhaps the clearest expression of the book's central thesis. The future enterprise will not be governed by perimeter walls alone. It will be governed by the quality of the identity, trust, and logic architecture embedded into every session, workflow, and relationship. The leader who prepares for that future now will not simply survive the next era of technical change. That leader will help define it.

The 2030 Leadership Mindset: The Infinite Architect

If the 2020s were defined by the pursuit of efficiency, the 2030s will be defined by the pursuit of resilience.

That shift is more than operational. It is civilized for leadership. In the earlier phase of intelligent systems adoption, much of the executive conversation focused on acceleration, productivity, automation, and cost compression. The question was how quickly the enterprise could adopt machine capability and convert it into measurable advantage. Those concerns were understandable, but they were also transitional. They belonged to the period when the organization was still learning to use intelligence as a tool.

The decade ahead demands something more mature. It demands that leadership move from deployment to stewardship, from implementation to endurance, and from static design to continuous governance. The architect leader can no longer think primarily in terms of projects with neat beginnings and endings. Intelligent systems are not projects in the traditional sense. They are living operational ecosystems. They evolve with data, with behavior, with incentives, with regulation, and with the changing realities of the institutions that rely on them. They are never simply finished.

This is why the 2030 roadmap requires a different mindset, the mindset of the *infinite architect.*

The infinite architect does not ask only whether the system works today. The infinite architect asks whether the system can remain governable tomorrow. The concern is no longer just implementation success. It is reflective governance, the disciplined practice of continuously examining whether the architecture is still aligned with mission, still secure under new conditions, still trustworthy under scale, and still bound by human values as autonomy expands.

That is one of the great lessons of this book. The vanity of the 2020s was the belief that intelligent systems could simply be controlled, contained, or mastered once and for all through policy, engineering, or executive will. The wisdom required for the 2030s is different. It is the recognition that leadership must increasingly partner with intelligence rather than merely command it. Not in the sense of surrendering human authority, but in the sense of accepting that the enterprise is now operating through systems dynamic enough that static control is no longer the right ambition.

What then anchors the leader in such a world.

The answer remains what it has always been, though now under new conditions: human values. Trust, dignity, sovereignty, accountability, fairness, proportionality, stewardship, and purpose become the North Star of the autonomous age. They are what allow partnership without drift, autonomy without moral collapse, and scale without dehumanization. The machine may carry the speed. The system may carry the complexity. But the leader must still carry the direction.

That is the leadership mindset of 2030. Not mastery through domination, but stewardship through architecture. Not confidence that the system will remain still, but discipline enough to govern it as it changes.

Conclusion: The Journey Beyond

This manuscript now comes to its end, but the mission it describes is only beginning.

What has been built across these chapters is not simply a framework for adopting new tools. It is a way of thinking about leadership in an era when intelligence has moved into the structure of the enterprise itself. The book has argued that the algorithm is not the center of the story. Architecture is. Governance is. Trust is. Identity is. Ethics is. Human judgment is. And above all, purpose is.

From the early challenge of seeing beyond the algorithm, to the rise of the architect leader, to the velocity of trust, to real time compliance, to workflow visibility, accountability, cloud strategy, session integrity, code literacy, ethical design, the augmented workforce, and the final scaling of the unscalable, one central theme has remained constant: the future belongs to leaders who can translate intelligence into institutionally worthy form.

That is why the 2030 roadmap is not merely a chapter ending. It is a call to action.

It is a reminder that the clarity achieved today is the foundation of the sovereignty exercised tomorrow. The organizations that endure will not be those that simply adopt intelligent systems first. They will be those that architect them wisely, govern them continuously, and align them with human ends worth serving. The future is not a force that merely arrives. It is an environment where leadership helps shape.

That is the deeper invitation of this book. Do not stand outside the transformation as a spectator. Do not reduce leadership to the management of technical acceleration. Become the architect of what intelligence is allowed to become within the enterprise, and through the enterprise, within the world.

The systems are running. The sessions are secure. The governance layer is alive. The roadmap is clear.

It is time to lead.

Bibliography

Note: These citations reflect the foundational technical standards, ethical frameworks, and philosophical texts that underpin the arguments made in Chapters 1 through 14.

Amazon Web Services. (2025). *AWS well-architected framework: Security pillar.* https://docs.aws.amazon.com/architecture/well-architected/

Anderson, R. (2020). *Security engineering: A guide to building dependable distributed systems* (3rd ed.). John Wiley & Sons.

Bostrom, N. (2014). *Superintelligence: Paths, dangers, strategies*. Oxford University Press.

Christian, B. (2020). *The alignment problem: Machine learning and human values*. W. W. Norton & Company.

Dignum, V. (2019). *Responsible artificial intelligence: How to develop and use AI in a responsible way*. Springer Nature.

Eaton, M. A. (1982). *Ecclesiastes: An introduction and commentary*. InterVarsity Press.

European Union. (2024). *Artificial Intelligence Act (Regulation (EU) 2024/1689)*. Official Journal of the European Union.

Microsoft Corporation. (2026). *Azure governance and compliance: Continuous control monitoring documentation.* https://learn.microsoft.com/en-us/azure/governance/

NIST. (2024). *Artificial intelligence risk management framework (AI RMF 1.0)*. National Institute of Standards and Technology.

Resseguier, A., & Rodrigues, R. (2020). AI ethics should not remain human-centric. *Ethics and Information Technology*, 22(4), 319–330.

Russell, S., & Norvig, P. (2020). *Artificial intelligence: A modern approach* (4th ed.). Pearson.

Schneier, B. (2018). *Click here to kill everybody: Security and survival in a hyper-connected world.* W. W. Norton & Company.

Van Rossum, G., & Drake, F. L. (2023). *Python 3.12 reference manual*. Python Software Foundation.

Zuboff, S. (2019). *The age of surveillance capitalism: The fight for a human future at the new frontier of power.* PublicAffairs.

The Architect-Leader's Checklist

This checklist serves as the operational core of the Beyond the Algorithm framework. Use it to audit any intelligent system before, during, and after deployment.

1. The Governance Layer (The GRC Core)

- [ ] **Real-Time Telemetry:** Does the system provide a live feed of compliance data, or are we relying on periodic snapshots?
- [ ] **Automated Assurance:** Are the "Logic Gates" hard-coded to reject non-compliant handshakes (e.g., RSA certificate mismatches) automatically?
- [ ] **The Kill Switch:** Is there a defined threshold where the system's "Machine Identity" is revoked instantly without human intervention?
- [ ] **Audit Fidelity:** Are all system logs immutable, timestamped, and stored in a centralized "Truth Engine" (Workflow Portal)?

2. Technical Integrity & Architecture

- [ ] **Sovereign Hybridity:** Can our core GRC logic move from Azure to AWS (or vice versa) in under 90 days if a provider's terms of service change?
- [ ] **Session Security:** Is mTLS (mutual Transport Layer Security) enforced on all machine-to-machine connections?

- [ ] **Cryptographic Resilience:** Have we inventoried our session plumbing for Quantum-Resistant readiness?
- [ ] **Code Transparency:** Can leadership perform a "Read-Only" review of the Python validation scripts to ensure they match corporate intent?

3. The Human-Machine Social Contract

- [ ] **HITL 2.0:** Have we removed the "Rubber Stamp" bottleneck? Does the system only escalate "Ambiguous" or "High-Impact" cases for human review?
- [ ] **The Reasoning Trace:** Does every AI-driven escalation include an Explainable AI (XAI) brief showing *why* the decision was made?
- [ ] **Risk Quantization:** Is risk expressed as a mathematical order of magnitude rather than a subjective color (Red/Yellow/Green)?
- [ ] **Augmented Literacy:** Has the workforce been trained to "Orchestrate" agents rather than "Execute" manual tasks?

4. Ethical Stewardship

- [ ] **The Ecclesiastes Test:** Does this automation serve a clear, human-centric mission, or is it merely "Vanity of Toil" (efficiency for efficiency's sake)?
- [ ] **Algorithmic Fairness:** Is there a recurring audit for "Logic Drift" or statistical bias in automated decision-making?

- [ ] **Sovereignty of Intent:** Are our organizational values the primary constraints of our code, or have we outsourced our ethics to the cloud provider's default settings?

www.ingramcontent.com/pod-product-compliance
Lightning Source LLC
LaVergne TN
LVHW091029080826
845145LV00002B/409

* 9 7 8 1 9 7 2 1 5 4 0 5 2 *